GOD'S MODEL FO[R]

DEED
&
TRUTH

JOURNAL

LA'WANA HARRIS

TABLE OF CONTENTS

INTRODUCTION

Welcome to the Deed & Truth Journal!

This journal is the companion guide for the *Faith Beyond Lip Service* book.

God gave us the power of love, the most disruptive idea the world has ever seen, and we are in need of a disruption. He gave us ultimate truth and the power of forgiveness and love for neighbor, brother, and even *enemies*. He gave us one baptism and a unifying Holy Spirit.

How have we stewarded these powerful gifts?

We have not made the most of what we've been given. As a Church and the race of humanity, we have not done our part yet in the continuation of this restoration project as the hands and the feet of the one who saved us to be ambassadors of peace and reconciliation. We have not preached a gospel of peace with God and peace between the nations.

We have not done what he left us here to do... not yet.

I invite you to explore with me some of the reasons why this is true and how we might go about remedying this. We know everything we need to know for peace on earth and good will to men. But do we know that we know? My hope is that this book will help us to know and act.

The love of Christ holds us together in unity. This guide is not meant to advocate for any one perspective or viewpoint other than what is written in scripture. Together we can navigate even the most polarizing topic or situation when we choose to follow Jesus' example.

Let's get started with our journey to commit in deed in truth.

The tools I will emphasize for operationalizing the principles in the book are found in what I call the **COMMIT Inclusive Behavior Framework**. The fuel for the framework for the Christian is the **Fruit of The Spirit** (Galatians 5:22-23)

Christ came into the world to offer salvation to everyone, with the intention that the local congregation should reflect that mindset. Embracing diversity, equity and inclusion is a part of God's divine plan for all people to receive salvation.

According to the Scriptures, everyone should be loved and welcomed into a caring body of believers. I invite you to move beyond words, beyond "lip service," to meaningful action that breaks the cycle of injustice and inequity that perpetrated in the body of Christ. We have an opportunity to not just ease into heaven while the world goes to hell in a handbasket. **We can COMMIT to being proactive in offering hope to our generation.**

I invite you to COMMIT to greater intentionality and action for DEI grounded in the unconditional love of Christ. You likely already have an opinion about DEI, since it is a hot topic in almost every sphere of our culture, including the Church. Maybe it has been a hot and divisive topic in your own church or around your own dinner table. My goal is to pull the rug out from under the satan's attempt to divide us before we even start the conversation. I hope to define terms, to point out possible blind spots, to offer some meat to all "sides" of the "conversation." I will show that there is actually no argument unless we create one. I am a Christian woman who is a Black and served as a DEI strategist to churches and organizations on every level in every sphere. I've thought a lot about this (an understatement), and I long to be helpful and share what I've learned for the glory of God and the good of the Church and the world.

In the book *Faith Beyond Lip Service*, I opened a dialogue with my fellow followers of Jesus Christ about a few fundamental questions.

What role do we play in honoring God's model for inclusion?

What does the Bible say about diversity, equity and inclusion?

What clues can we decipher from God's creativity?

How do we move forward in solidarity?

What specific actions should we take to be the hands and feet of Christ?

Instead of being told at a secular DEI training session that you need to be "more inclusive" and to make sure everyone can recite a DEI statement, *Faith Beyond Lip Service* supports you in developing your insights about DEI from Christ's example.

There's no hidden agenda or propaganda—just love.

THE COMMIT FRAMEWORK

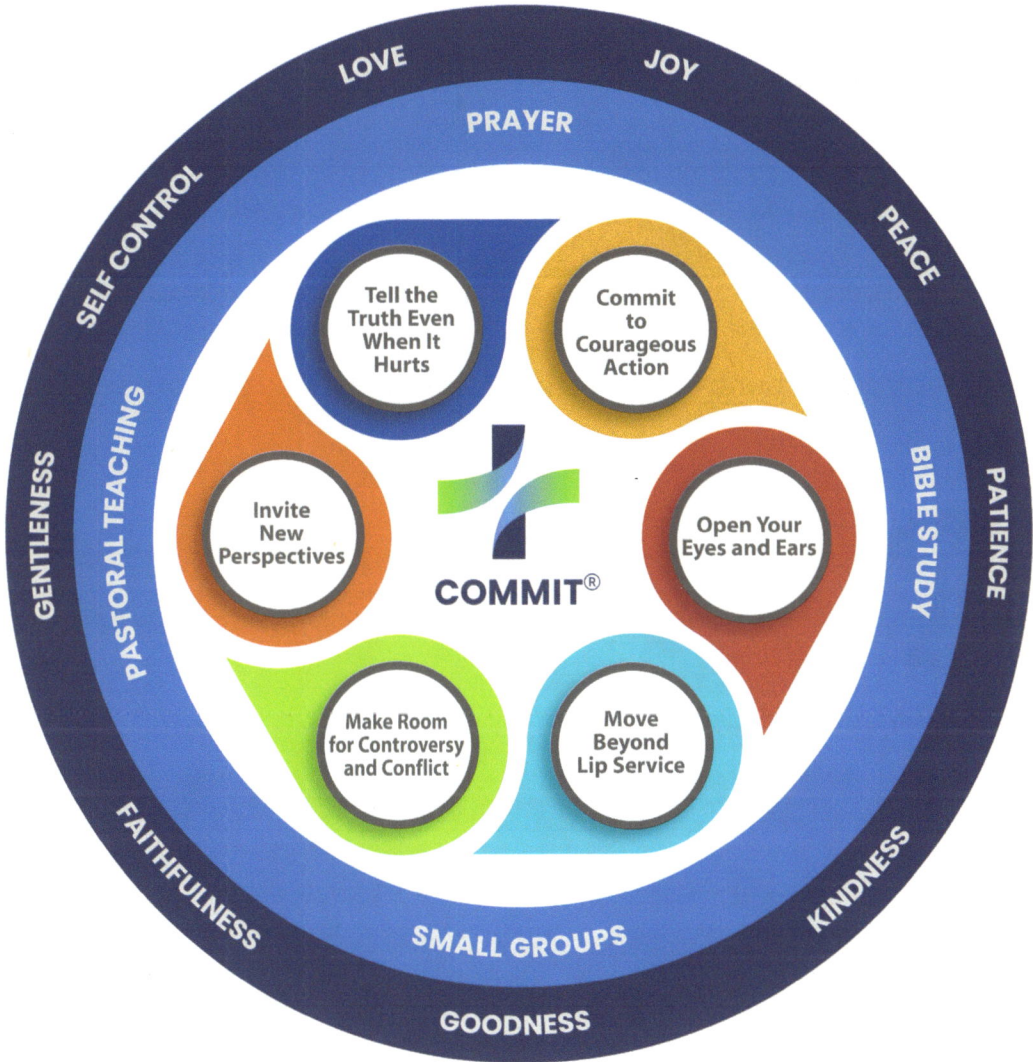

The COMMIT Inclusive Behavior Framework brings structure to the faith-based DEI conversation by providing a blueprint for building a mindset and environment where we honor God's model for inclusion without compromising our faith. To COMMIT, means to:

9

Commit to Courageous Action (for family, church, the world)	**Open Your Eyes and Ears (to the good, the bad, and the ugly)**	**Move Beyond Lip Service**
Make Room for Controversy and Conflict	**Invite New Perspectives**	**Tell the Truth Even When it Hurts**

While the inclusive behaviors sound (and are) simple, they are not necessarily easy.

1 Start with Christ in the center, represented by the cross.

2 Prayerfully COMMIT to biblical DEI principles with the six inclusive behaviors.

3 Share your questions and thoughts using the Deed & Truth Journal to help guide faith-based DEI discussions with your prayer group.

4 Deepen your ability to understand, evangelize, and disciple people from all walks of life by demonstrating the fruit of the spirit in your everyday interactions.

CHRIST-CENTERED DEI PROCESS

The process for demonstrating Christ-centered DEI:

The *Deed & Truth Journal* is designed for individuals, families, small groups, and congregations. Follow the steps outlined below for a Christ-centered biblical approach to addressing complicated and polarizing issues related to DEI.

1. PRAY	Seek the Lord in your prayer time for how to best honor His model of inclusion in your heart, in your home, in your church and in discipleship in the world.
2. CONNECT	Make sure all your efforts are centered in sound biblical teaching from your local pastor and supported in your prayer circle, small groups or bible study.
3. COMMIT	Practice the COMMIT framework for a faith-based approach to DEI.
4. ENGAGE	Focus on demonstrating the Fruit of the Spirit daily so that you do not feel you have to choose between secular ideology and biblical principles.
5. DISCIPLE	Welcome new believers and new seekers into the Kingdom of God. We are called to win the world for Christ.

Making the effort to understand the mindset and specific actions needed to serve with a spirit of excellence is a matter of choice. Thankfully, The Apostle Paul gives us a clear blueprint to work from in 1 Corinthians 9:22-23.

To the weak I became weak, to win the weak. I have become all things to all people so that by all possible means I might save some. I do all this for the sake of the gospel, that I may share in its blessings. (1 Cor 9:22)

The Message bible puts it this way.

Even though I am free of the demands and expectations of everyone, I have voluntarily become a servant to any and all in order to reach a wide range of people: religious, nonreligious, meticulous moralists, loose-living immoralists, the defeated, the demoralized—whoever. I didn't take on their way of life. I kept my bearings in Christ—but I entered their world and tried to experience things from their point of view. I've become just about every sort of servant there is in my attempts to lead those I meet into a God-saved life. I did all this because of the Message. I didn't just want to talk about it; I wanted to be in on it! (1 Cor 9:22)

FOUNDATIONAL PRINCIPLES

Keep these foundational principles in mind as you read the devotions and have discussions with fellow believers.

1. Christ above All – Diversity, equity, and inclusion is not about "wokeness." They are, rather, additional ways of becoming more like Christ and fulfilling his mandate to make disciples of all nations. I do this work out of my passion and reverence for Christ. Heaven is going to be the divine example of a diverse, equitable and inclusive church. It's time to bring some of God's sovereign design for the body of Christ in this world.

2. God loves to take things that we don't understand and do something miraculous – Do you think people understood the Messiah in a manger? Do you think the man born blind understood his high calling to glorify God? Or did Abraham have any idea when God called him up to the mountain with his own son as the sacrifice, that, no, it would be God alone who would sacrifice his Son so that all others could be saved? God will do something miraculous, especially with those things we don't understand.

3. We are God's plan for a time such as this – If you find yourself praying that God would make the body of Christ more unified and that his Church would lead the way in the ministry of reconciliation across the globe, then it's a good prayer, just so long as we remember that we are also God's answer to our prayer. We help non-believers be reconciled to God and believers be reconciled to one another.

The ministry of reconciliation requires active participation from every believer. One plants; one waters, and God gives the increase (1 Corinthians 3:7). As we proclaim the gospel, we act as peacemakers, and invite God's blessings (Matthew 5:9). When we share and live out His message of reconciliation, lives are changed, and God gets the glory.

WEEK 1: COMMIT TO COURAGEOUS ACTION (for family, church, the world)

QUOTABLES

When God speaks, oftentimes His voice will call for an act of courage on our part.

— Charles Stanley

WEEK 1: COMMIT TO COURAGEOUS ACTION (for family, church, the world)

As a believer, we understand that our entire existence and the blessings we enjoy today are linked to the courageous action of one man, Jesus Christ. He took the bold step to accept to carry the burden of our sin, suffer humiliation and excruciating pain and torture, and experience a gruesome death for us to be saved and then live.

Before Jesus saved you, you were oppressed by the devil, excluded from God's presence because He is too holy to behold iniquity, and then condemned to suffering and death.

Take a cursory look at your life before what Jesus did for you. You will see that your condition was like that of immigrants denied access to opportunities and people who suffer discrimination because of their race, beliefs, gender, and ethnicity. Yet, despite all these, one man, Jesus, stood beside you to make things right and accept you.

No better courageous action can be compared to what Jesus has done for you on the Cross at Calvary. He committed to this courageous action without bothering about your status as a sinner. Instead, His genuine love for you qualified you and made you worthy of receiving His love and mercy. So now you are sanctified and qualified to be called His own. "But God demonstrates His own love toward us, in that while we were still sinners, Christ died for us" (Romans 5:8).

Consequently, God's gift of salvation comes with a responsibility - you must deliberately commit to courageous action for others, including your family, church, and the world. Jesus says in Mark 12:31 that you should "love your neighbor as yourself."

To love is a command and an action. You cannot say you love a God who you cannot see with your physical eyes if you do not love those around you (1 John 4:20). Also, you cannot say you love people if you do not demonstrate it consistently.

Demonstrating your love for people takes courage, especially when it seems difficult to love that person. Likewise, it takes courage to stand alone in a world riddled with discrimination, inequity, and marginalization.

However, you have been called to be a light in a world clouded with darkness. Jesus has saved you so that you can invite others into the Kingdom of God. He has comforted you so you can do the same for others. Your voice should echo positivity and love in a room full of negativity and hate. In a world full of bad news—you can share the good news of Jesus Christ.

In your journey toward imbibing the habit of taking courageous actions, remember you don't have to know everything to positively impact people and your environment. All you need to do is to obey God's calling, trust the Holy Spirit's leading and rely on God's provision.

Now that you know that God is counting on you to take a stand, embrace diversity, equity, and inclusion as designed by our sovereign creator, and appreciate all people by committing to courageous actions— how do you begin?

LOOK AROUND YOU

Saving the world begins with taking one courageous step in your immediate environment and within your circle of influence. It's time to shift focus from doing big things to appreciating the small acts of courage to correct certain behaviors and actions within your power daily.

For example, what do you say when someone tells an offensive joke at the dinner table, not knowing the new neighbors you invited are immigrants?

Or, what do you do if your church is invited to join a city-wide faith coalition and one of the leaders says, "We don't go to that side of town"?

Imagine a situation where the world is enraged with senseless violence, and people in your congregation and the broader community look to your church for refuge and direction; how do you engage?

Sometimes it can be intimidating to take a stand for Christ, especially in situations where people have differing and strong opinions. But that's God's specialty. Jesus was not popular or widely accepted based on his ministry at a time when the religious tradition was being challenged.

To commit to courageous action based on sound biblical principles, we must carefully discern God's commands versus man's beliefs.

For example, God's Word encourages us in Proverbs 31:8-9 to "Speak up for those who cannot speak for themselves, for the rights of all who are destitute. Speak up and judge fairly; defend the rights of the poor and needy."

The place you are right now is a platform you must use to speak against injustice and unfairness, correct, and sometimes express sharp disapproval because of people's behavior or actions.

Doing this might be difficult because it might mean speaking

18

against your family, friends, or church members. But no one says it's going to be easy. If it was, the Bible wouldn't emphasize the need for you to "be courageous; be strong" (1 Corinthians 16:13).

However, you must learn to apply love and patience when correcting people. Many people need to realize that what they are doing is wrong. People act better when they know better. Therefore, make it your responsibility to show people how and why we must love everyone as believers.

LEAD WITH COMPASSION

Jesus' earthly ministry is a practical example of compassion's power and why every believer must express it to everyone.

Compassion is the expression of sympathy, pity, and concern for the sufferings or ills of others. We see Jesus always compassionate toward people that need help with their physical, emotional, and spiritual needs. Compassion was a major ingredient in Jesus' miraculous ministry.

In Luke 7:13 and Matthew 15:32, respectively, Jesus was propelled by compassion to raise the dead son of a widow and feed the crowd. He didn't care if they were Jews or Greek, male or female. All He saw were people desperately in need, and He acted.

If there's no room for compassion in your heart, it will be difficult to take any courageous action. Therefore, you must be concerned about people's plights and sufferings before you will be able to do an act of kindness to them.

If you find yourself in a position where you can help someone, kindly do so without asking too many questions. Jesus wouldn't minister to the people while they were hungry. He fed them first (John 6:1-11).

He didn't ask the people who were hungry and without any food, "why have you come here without provisions?" Or "what have you done to try to get your own food?" Or "why should this child have to share his food with all of these able-bodied adults?"

- ______
- ______
- ______
- ______

Can you learn from this by focusing on others' needs and problems and not who they are, what they represent, or what people think about them?

- ______
- ______
- ______
- ______

For example, can you change your perspective to be, "It doesn't matter why someone is hungry; let's just get them something to eat, and we can sort out the rest later?"

- ______
- ______
- ______
- ______

Committing to courageous action will become easy as you allow God to fill your heart with compassion towards people and purge you of every spirit of selfishness, making you turn a blind eye to the predicaments of others.

DISCERN THE "BOOTSTRAP" MINDSET

The bootstrap mindset believes that people can pull themselves out of their own predicaments only if they work harder or do something about their conditions. It pushes the ideology that people should be self-made and achieve their dreams alone.

The bootstrap mindset sounds like some heroic act, but the reality is that most people cannot rise unless someone gives them a helping hand. No one is self-made. Everyone, at some point, has been given an opportunity or platform to thrive and excel.

We cannot ignore the fact that some people enjoy immense privileges and opportunities by being citizens of a nation, particularly a first-world country, belonging to a particular race, and being members of a specific family. Therefore, rising to the top is easy because society and family have given them leverage.

Unfortunately, others don't enjoy these benefits. They will barely rise and become successful even when they toil daily because many odds are against them.

This was the situation of the sick man at the pool that had an encounter with Jesus in John 5:1-9. His condition made him disadvantaged. Others got to the pool before him and got their healing while he remained in a spot for many years.

Many other sick people who had more privilege than him would wonder why he didn't get his healing. After all, they were all sick before they managed to jump into the pool. But his case was worse, which made him extremely slow or immobile until Jesus healed him.

Many people grab hold of the "take up your bed and walk" portion of John 5:8 but ignore the fact that Jesus had to act before his bones received strength and his body healing to rise.

It would help if you consciously chose to lean in with compassion as a believer. You must understand that God has placed us above so we can pull people out of their sinking sand situations.

You are on a rescue mission to save people from inequality and give them leverage. You are a rescuer responsible for rescuing people drowning in the river of lack of opportunities, discrimination, and hardship and helping them stay afloat.

Do not allow the "pull yourself up by your own bootstraps" sentiment to hinder you from taking courageous actions when someone needs your help. 1 John 3:17 asks a crucial rhetorical question, "But whoever has this world's goods, and sees his brother in need, and shuts up his heart from him, how does the love of God abide in him?"

The measure of God's love in your heart is determined by your willingness to become a launchpad that will elevate someone else, especially the underprivileged.

Assessment

I am committed to taking action to honor God's plan for inclusion at home, in church, and the world. _____

I listen with empathy and do not interrupt others to help build genuine relationships. _____

I fellowship with people with different cultures, backgrounds, and thought processes. _____

I pray for ways to better adapt and connect with people that hold different values and beliefs for the cause of Christ. _____

I lead with courage and initiate actions or conversations about inclusion when I encounter words or actions that hurt others. _____

What are your areas of strength? How have they shown up in your life?

❈ _____

❈ _____

What are your areas of opportunity? How have they shown up in your life?

❈ _____

❈ _____

APPLICATION

SELF

> For each strength, identify a specific action you can take toward faith-based inclusion.

> For each area of opportunity, identify a specific action you can take toward greater inclusion.

> Pray about your action plan with your spouse or prayer partner and share your experiences.

HOME

> Encourage your family to take the COMMIT self-assessment and identify their strengths and areas of opportunity.

> Create a safe space for family members to share their experiences, questions, and challenges relative to DEI.

> Integrate the COMMIT model when having conversations about DEI to help move forward in solidarity.

CHURCH

> Join or take a leadership role in one of your church's outreach fellowship/ministry.

> Make inclusive ministry, evangelism, and discipleship a priority to best meet the needs of those you are called to serve. Don't assume; ask people if they feel included and belong.

> Incorporate Christ's examples for addressing DEI when teaching about how to minister in new places.

24

PRAYER

Commit to Courageous Action
- Joshua 1:9

Dear Lord, You commanded me in Your Word to be strong and of good courage. Therefore, I ask that You give me the courage to commit to courageous actions even amidst fear and opposition. Help me to show love, care and kindness to everyone I come across, irrespective of their background, race, religion gender or any other aspect of their identity. In Jesus' name, Amen.

Reflection

What specific areas will you pray about from this week's lesson?

- ______________________________
- ______________________________
- ______________________________
- ______________________________
- ______________________________

What specific actions will you take to move Godward?

- ______________________________
- ______________________________
- ______________________________
- ______________________________
- ______________________________

Capture your thoughts in the notes section.

Notes

�֍ _____

�֍ _____

✷ _____

✷ _____

✷ _____

✷ _____

✷ _____

✷ _____

✷ _____

✷ _____

✷ _____

✷ _____

✷ _____

✷ _____

✷ _____

✷ _____

WEEK 2: OPEN YOUR EYES AND EARS (to the good, the bad, and the ugly)

QUOTABLES

*The wider you open your mind
to embrace diversity, the better
picture of God you have.*

— TD Jakes

WEEK 2: OPEN YOUR EYES AND EARS (to the good, the bad, and the ugly)

The apostle Paul prayed a simple but profound prayer in Ephesians 1:17-18a, "that the God of our Lord Jesus Christ, the Father of glory, may give to you the spirit of wisdom and revelation in the knowledge of Him, the eyes of your understanding being enlightened."

The eyes Paul was referring to in this prayer are not the physical ones. Instead, he was talking about the eyes of your heart that sees and understands the pain and struggle of people around you and respond to them.

Similarly, just as God hears the cry of your heart even without you voicing your needs and challenges, you must also sharpen your inner ears to the plight of others.

There's so much going on in people's lives, including yours. Your needs, dreams, and aspirations can become a veil stopping you from seeing the realities of others' struggles. Your thoughts and internal wishes can also become so noisy that you might not hear the whispers of the hurting and the desperate.

We are living in desperate times. Depression, sicknesses, and hardship in all areas are climaxing. Things are happening fast, and situations are deteriorating quickly like never before. For other people, it is even worse based on conditions beyond their control, like skin color, sex, ethnicity, etc. The burden is twice as heavy as for others. Therefore, their more prone to crumble under the heavy weight of personal and general issues.

However, you are made for such a time like this. The Bible says in Matthew 5:16, "Let your light so shine before men, that they may see your good works and glorify your Father in heaven."

What other time is light needed than in a world where the shadows of darkness seem to be spreading fast? God has prepared you to be more sensitive in the spirit, with sharpened senses, discerning issues and problems and responding to them as a change agent.

But you cannot achieve this calling if your eyes and ears cannot see and hear the good, bad, and ugly around you.

THE GOOD

Firstly, you must understand your mandate as a Christian, which is to spread the Good News. The Good News is the Gospel of Christ that preaches hope, love, and life.

The world is in desperate need of this message, and Jesus Christ has charged you in Matthew 28:19-20 to teach people across the globe about Christ and what He represents, helping them to experience the transformational love of God and choosing a better path in life that leads to total freedom and unlimited blessings.

You have the Good News of the Gospel to share daily in a world that faces a tsunami of bad news. You can choose to be open to see and hear what the Holy Spirit is saying about God's will for a time such as these. God's Word says the Holy Spirit is your teacher, who teaches all things and a guide giving you explicit information about what and what not to do (John 14:26, Isaiah 30:21).

Relying on the Holy Spirit by deliberately opening your eyes and ears would make you experience an outburst of insight from Him that will help you be a better person to others.

Life is hard, scary, and confusing, and the Bible foretells what is happening now. Unfortunately, some days it's hard to differentiate between the headlines at the top of the news cycle and biblical prophecy for the last days.

However, God has already given us the victory through His Son, Jesus Christ. He says in His Word, *"These things I have spoken to you that in Me you may have peace. In the world you will have tribulation, but be of good cheer; I have overcome the world"* (John 16:33).

God's Word is complete and has solutions to every problem. Therefore, many of the answers you need to navigate this world with so many different people, backgrounds, and cultures can be found by searching and living the scripture with your faith community. Searching the scriptures will open your mind to see what God has for you and His promises that never fail.

Also, you must be willing to go outside your circle and the familiar faces around you and learn from people with different experiences. You gain so much when you open your heart to learn from others. So step aside from the familiar and greet everyone you meet with an open heart to know and understand new perspectives about life.

THE BAD

Unfortunately, death and calamity run rampant in our society. But we must work on how we perceive and respond to tragic societal events. For instance, why is our first response to the debate that a person or group deserved to suffer in a tragic event instead of the natural, human response of empathy for a life that's been lost or left devastated?

You can lessen the impact of bad situations on people if you choose to be more solution-oriented, compassionate, and empathetic. You must understand that we are connected together, and the pain of one person is a pain to all.

I spent years working in an indigent clinic providing direct patient care to the homeless and uninsured in Greensboro, North Carolina, during the height of the AIDS epidemic. But, then, so much misinformation was circulating around about how to contract, manage and treat the disease.

My proximity to the epidemic and its impacts was about as close as I could get as a medical professional. For example, I was pretty good at what we called "hard sticks," referring to people with small veins that were hard to find. I was often called away from the doctor I was working with to assist in the lab after the phlebotomist had unsuccessfully tried to collect blood several times. I remember the sheer terror I and others felt from the occasional accidental finger prick when disposing of a used needle in such a dense population of patients living with AIDS.

I also witnessed first-hand people being treated as modern-day lepers. It was hard to make sense of the harsh treatment of an entire population living with a devastating disease. I felt immense pain as I sat at a hospice facility in a dimly lit room across from someone so young with full-blown AIDS suffering in the last hours of their life. It was overwhelming. That night watching and praying for him as he transitioned was one of the many experiences that fueled my passion for change. He was more than a patient taking his last breath—he was a soul entering eternity.

The impetus for my desire to see the body of Christ open its eyes and ears to the many ways we're called to serve in an imperfect world comes from a profound visceral place of life-altering experiences.

I've seen the ugly up close and personal, and I'm confident that the love of God will help us all. The church is not a building. The church is a body of believers, followers of Jesus Christ—people—united for the glory of God. Christ said to the church in Matthew 25:35-40 that whatever we do to the vulnerable amongst us, we do it to Him. *"Assuredly, I say to you, inasmuch as you did it to one of the least of these My brethren, you did it to Me."*

There's little one person can do. But when the church is united in love and purpose, it can cause a revolution, and people's lives will be touched and saved.

Just like during the AIDS epidemic, the world is still nursing its wounds from the global pandemic. What are you doing to help people survive the impact of the lockdown and other covid-19 related issues?
Bad things will never stop happening in this world. But if you choose to sharpen your eyes and ears to see and hear people in desperate need, the world

will recover quickly from any challenge.

THE UGLY

It is no longer news that the church is constantly persecuted. This has been the case from Bible days when the church faced stiff opposition from people who could not tolerate the truth of the Gospel and could not withstand the heat of the truth. As a result, Jesus and His disciples were all persecuted, and almost all of them experienced gruesome deaths.

The ugly truth is that the church is still battling this challenge. Churches in nations around the world are passing through various forms of attack, from suffering direct destruction of people's lives and property to the government enacting obnoxious policies to hinder the expansion of the church and spread of the good news.

However, that is the most popular form of persecution. There is another form of persecution that is subtle but more lethal. It is that which is perpetrated by "the church."

As bizarre as it may sound, the so-called church has harmed many people, all in the name of trying to share their views or truth. Many people have condemned and abused many people under the guise of preaching the gospel. They have hurt people's feelings and done directly opposite what Jesus preaches and what the church stands for.

We have seen certain groups and factions that have wreaked havoc with their own hate-filled actions in the guise of fulfilling their Christian duty. They uphold misogynistic, racist, and classist ideologies and cause great devastation. They have the "holier than thou" mindset, claiming self-righteousness while condemning people for being different.

The bottom line is that people that call themselves "the church" have found themselves on the right and wrong side of history at various times. And we can't ignore that. We can't skip the parts of history that are not favorable to us or our narrative.

However, we can't harp on specific aspects of history to the point that it immobilizes us and keeps us from moving forward. As believers, the best thing to do is to introspect and reconsider our ways deeply. Then, we can retrace our steps and go back on the right track.

Jesus' earthly ministry must be our template. Just as He went about people's homes, cities, and villages doing good, we must ensure we become forces of changing, moving from one heart to the other, ministering peace to the troubled and hope to the downcast. Jesus never discriminates. He never cared whether a person was righteous or not. All He was interested in was reaching out to souls and transforming their lives. When He met the Samaritan woman who had been married five times and was cohabiting with another, Jesus never called her names

(John 4:1-42). Instead, He offered her the living water.

The church cannot afford to contribute to the pain in society today. We must embrace all people, no matter who they are. We must be non-judgmental and less critical. We must submit ourselves to God and allow Him to work in our lives, transforming our hearts by removing the stony hearts and replacing them with the heart of flesh.

You are responsible for opening your eyes and ears to see and know about the ugly trends that might be cropping up in the church. You must speak against them with wisdom and backing of God's Word to cut off the spread of evil coming from the hearts of religious people who have not experienced God's genuine love and the regeneration of their minds and spirit.

ALWAYS ASK YOURSELF

What aspects of this situation am I not familiar with based on my lived experience?

※ ______________________________

※ ______________________________

※ ______________________________

※ ______________________________

※ ______________________________

Are diversity, equity, and inclusion just a state of being, or are there material and spiritual benefits to this kind of worldview, mindset, and church culture?

※ ______________________________

※ ______________________________

※ ______________________________

※ ______________________________

※ ______________________________

Are more souls discipled in when believers and churches operate with an inclusive mindset/culture?

※ ______________________________

※ ______________________________

※ ______________________________

※ ______________________________

※ ______________________________

Will the body of Christ grow faster?

�֎ _____

✖ _____

✖ _____

✖ _____

✖ _____

✖ _____

Does the impact of the ministry become more dynamic?

✖ _____

✖ _____

✖ _____

✖ _____

✖ _____

✖ _____

Is there greater trust from the communities the church is called to serve?

✖ _____

✖ _____

✖ _____

✖ _____

✖ _____

✖ _____

Assessment

RATE EACH STATEMENT USING THE FOLLOWING:
5 Strongly Agree
4 Agree
3 Neutral
2 Disagree
1 Strongly Disagree

I am comfortable articulating the value of faith-based inclusion for myself, my home, and my church. _____

I listen to the people, communities, and countries I/we are called to serve to understand their needs. _____

I pray for revelation and discernment concerning my blind spots and biases about people with different backgrounds and values. _____

I seek to learn about cultures and backgrounds different from my own. _____

I try to understand the source of my discomfort when faced with challenging situations. _____

What are your areas of strength? How have they shown up in your life?

❋ _____

❋ _____

What are your areas of opportunity? How have they shown up in your life?

❋ _____

❋ _____

APPLICATION

SELF

> Be intentional about understanding the experience of people with different backgrounds and values.

> Establish a discipleship relationship with someone different from you.

> Pay attention to your inner voice, preferences, and patterns in your interactions with others different from you.

HOME

> Create a "Missions" segment for your bible study or prayer group to increase awareness and connection to different cultures.

> Establish a relationship and support for a missionary in another country to learn more about the people they serve.

> Open a dialogue with members from different generations to learn from each other's experiences.

CHURCH

> Pray about and apply a faith-based DEI lens when engaging in underserved communities with diverse backgrounds and experiences.

> Ensure diverse representation when making key ministry decisions that impact communities/countries different from your leadership and congregation. Go beyond "diversity of thought" to include local pastors and lay members who know the community. People need to see someone that looks like them on your ministry team.

> Understand that it is God that gives us the desire and the power to do what pleases Him. (Philippians 2:13) This awareness helps us avoid the savior complex and give all glory to God.

PRAYER

Open your Eyes and Ears
- 1 John 3:17

Heavenly Father, open my eyes to see the needs of people around me. Open my ears to hear their cry. Touch my mind to be moved by compassion toward them. Help me not to shut the door of my heart against them. Instead, let Your love in me lead me to give them from the resources You have blessed me with. Help me to restore their hope again. In Jesus' name, Amen.

Reflection

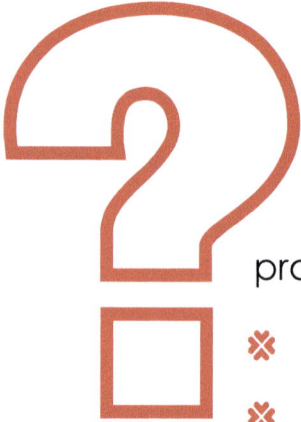

What specific areas will you
pray about from this week's lesson?

❋ _____

❋ _____

❋ _____

❋ _____

❋ _____

What specific actions will you
take to move Godward?

❋ _____

❋ _____

❋ _____

❋ _____

❋ _____

Capture your thoughts in the
notes section.

Notes

�֍ _____

�֍ _____

✷ _____

✷ _____

✷ _____

✷ _____

✷ _____

✷ _____

✷ _____

✷ _____

✷ _____

✷ _____

✷ _____

✷ _____

✷ _____

✷ _____

WEEK 3: MOVE BEYOND LIP SERVICE

QUOTABLES

*"It is not about reading the Word.
It is about obeying the Word."*

— Joyce Meyer

WEEK 3: MOVE BEYOND LIP SERVICE

You are not a churchgoer. You are the church. This sounds like a cliche, but it is the truth. Understanding and accepting that you are the church and not a building you visit for service will improve your life as a Christian and a valuable member of society.

We live in a world where people form a perception about you just by the way you live your life. You do not have to communicate or relate with them. All they do is observe how you treat others and behave, and then they reach a conclusion about the kind of person you are.

Doing that may come off as judgmental or biased, but that is the reality of our world. People address people based on their physical appearance and actions, not what they say.

Why does this matter to you as a believer? One of the most vocal sets of people are Christians. We regularly hold church services preaching the Gospel of Christ. We are also on the streets evangelizing. We visit prisons, hospitals, orphanage homes, etc., to share good tidings about the love of Christ and try to make people accept Christ and renounce their old lifestyles.

But in many cases, we need to practice what we preach. As a result, we often confuse people because while our lips are preaching and singing, our actions are judging, abusing, and criticizing.

Some people switch personalities like they are changing clothing. They are friendly and warm within the four walls of the church but are unapproachable and hostile in their homes, offices, and neighborhoods. They maintain a double-standard lifestyle and do not practice what they preach.

Jesus calls people whose words from their lips do not tally with their lifestyle hypocrites. *"These people draw near to Me with their mouth, and honor Me with their lips, but their heart is far from Me"* (Matthew 15:8). These are the churchgoers who never miss a service but have questionable characters. As a result, they discriminate and marginalize people who do not worship in their church or do not believe their doctrines.

God's Word commands us always to practice what we read in the scriptures. Here's what James 1:22-25 say about doing God's Word

"But be doers of the word, and not hearers only, deceiving yourselves. For if anyone is a hearer of the word and not a doer, he is like a man observing his natural face in a mirror, for he observes himself, goes away, and immediately forgets what kind of man he was.

But he who looks into the perfect law of liberty and continues in it, and is not a forgetful hearer but a doer of the work, this one will be blessed in what he does."

You become transformed and blessed when you practice what you preach and read in your Bible. That is the only way you can impact lives and draw people to Christ. People need to be the church, not just go to church. The church is not somewhere you go; it's who you are.

LOVE IS THE ANSWER

One thing that can make you move from mere lip service to actual action is genuine love for people. Love is a powerful force that can propel you to defend, help, provide for people and commit to positive actions that will benefit your immediate environment and the world at large.

We see what happened in John 3:16. The Bible says God so loved the world. But that was not all. He proved His love by giving His one and only precious Son, Jesus Christ, to come and die for sinners.

In that verse of the Bible, God's Words and His action corresponded. He did not only say He loved the world, but He proved it by sending someone who would deliver sinners from the consequences of sin, including death.

God's love does not discriminate. His salvation plan involves the entire human race. He doesn't care what your race, ethnicity, sexual orientation, and beliefs are; He loves everyone equally and doesn't want anyone to perish.

We must be like God. We must move from claiming God's love in our hearts to living in love. People must be able to distinguish us from others by our actions.

"By this all will know that you are My disciples, if you have love for one another" (John 13:35). Love is stronger than religion and more potent than any sermon you preach. People are increasingly becoming selfish and self-centered. No one cares about the poor and less privileged. Everyone is running towards achieving one goal or the other without factoring others into their plans. Jesus is telling His disciples that love is all that matters beyond the healings, teachings, and deliverances they would do.

1 Corinthians 13:1-8 stresses the futility of gifts, talent, and great works without love. Verse 1-3 says, *"Though I speak with the tongues of men and of angels, but have not love, I have become sounding brass or a clanging cymbal. And though I have the gift of prophecy, and understand all mysteries and all knowledge, and though I have all faith, so that I could remove mountains, but have not love, I am nothing. And though I bestow all my goods to feed the poor, and though I give my body to be burned, but have not love, it profits me nothing."*

However, verses 4-7 tell us what love means. *"Love suffers long and is kind; love does not envy;*

love does not parade itself, is not puffed up; does not behave rudely, does not seek its own, is not provoked, thinks no evil; does not rejoice in iniquity, but rejoices in the truth; bears all things, believes all things, hopes all things, endures all things."

These verses summarize the purpose of the church and its duty to society. The church must deal with people with kindness and patience, enduring others' weaknesses and completing them where they are lacking. The church should love in humility, upholding the truth and enduring the differences in people without complaining.

Love never fails. The things you say are fleeting; your thoughts are invisible and do not matter. But the good things you do for people, even the least, will leave a lasting impact in people's lives and the world (1 Corinthians 13:8). Love is the answer.

Christianity is not synonymous with conservative or liberal political views. The language of the church is love. The church must always engage in civil discourse with a voice of hope and love, not criticism and hate. We can co-create a path forward in solidarity without finger-pointing blame or shame.

LEAD IN DEED AND TRUTH

"Dear children, let us not love with words or speech but with actions and in truth." (1 John 3:18)
I'll be transparent and vulnerable. At first, I wrestled with God about writing this book. Then, I tried the Moses "not me" approach when God told him to tell Pharoah to let his people go.

"But Moses pleaded with the LORD, "O Lord, I'm not very good with words. I never have been, and I'm not now, even though you have spoken to me. I get tongue-tied, and my words get tangled." (Exodus 4:10)

I rattled off the stereotypical mantras around credentials, gender, race, and age as reasons someone else would be better suited to bring this message to the world. However, it wasn't until I realized that these thoughts were not actually my thoughts. Instead, they were planted as seeds by the media and individuals who want to uphold the status quo for which voices deserve to be heard and respected.

So, I put on my big girl pants and sought seasoned Godly counsel for how to bring about this message with integrity and biblical truth.

It was no longer enough for me to talk about these issues with my friends, family, and fellow believers in a bubble. It's time to move beyond lip service to meaningful action.

The messages we send through the people we put in positions of leadership, whose voice is amplified and whose voice is muted, can impact a person's perception of themselves. Therefore, you must be intentional about what you say and do because people are always watching you. You're the living Bible people read before picking up their hard copy or digital Bibles. So, reflect God's Word in a positive light.

You must also understand that you do not need a title or platform to lead. Everyone is a leader in different capacities in their lives. Whether in your office, home, church, or neighborhood, there's always someone looking up to you for direction and inspiration. You are a leader to that person. And you must understand that you hold tremendous power over that person because your actions and inactions can influence them and the decisions they will make now and in the future.

You must ensure that your deeds inspire and not discourage positive changes. You must preach the truth and adhere to your principles and teachings.

When Jesus was teaching His disciples about humility and servant-leadership in John 13:1-17, He did not only give an inspirational and thought-provoking speech. Instead, He got that on His knees, took a bowl of water, washed the dusty feet of His disciples, and cleaned them with a towel.

Here is what Jesus said to His disciples in John 13:15 after washing their feet, *"I have given you an example, that you should do as I have done to you."* Jesus had the confidence to say this because He led in deed and truth, not only by lips or speech.

We desire to be like Jesus. Our actions need to match your words. We must be humble when dealing with people, especially people society shuns. We can inspire them to meaningful action when we lead by example.

Live with the consciousness that you are shaping people's mindsets daily, and what you do today will potentially be a reference point when they want to make a decision tomorrow.

Look around your church, your ministries, your home. What messages are you sending? There are intended and unintended consequences for your actions and the messages you convey.

WHAT NEXT?

Now is the time to act and let people feel your impact. Do not wait for a title to be conferred on you before you begin to lead in action and truth and show love. Every day is an opportunity to be good and kind. Everywhere you find yourself is a platform to demonstrate what it means to care for someone.

Therefore, just as Jesus commanded His disciples to be His witness from Judea to Samaria and to the end of the earth (Acts 1:8), you must go into the world, to the places where people are suffering various forms of discrimination. You must reach out to them and save them.

Remember, unlike privilege, a byproduct of the social construct of race and capitalism, salvation truly is universally accessible and available for all. But you have the responsibility to reach out your hands to the unsaved. You can become the channel through which Jesus' message of love will spread to the four corners of the earth.

It's time to move beyond words as we grow in our faith. The time is now.

Assessment

RATE EACH STATEMENT USING THE FOLLOWING:
5 Strongly Agree
4 Agree
3 Neutral
2 Disagree
1 Strongly Disagree

I welcome every day as an opportunity to see the inherent value in every person I meet as a part of God's creation. ____________

I set expectations for creating an inclusive environment with my family and church while modeling inclusive behaviors. ____________

I prioritize the Great Commission and the benefit of a person's soul over any worldly event or topic. ____________

I address stereotypes that can negatively affect ministry and evangelism environments. ____________

I lead by example by using my voice to encourage respect for all of God's creation and invite my family and friends to do the same. ____________

What are your areas of strength? How have they shown up in your life?

- ____
- ____

What are your areas of opportunity? How have they shown up in your life?

- ____
- ____

APPLICATION

SELF

> Speak up in love at social gatherings, meetings and conferences when exclusionary behaviors show up in comments and actions.

> Identify the unique blessings in your life and pray about how you can use them to lift up others.

> Ask the Lord to give you divine assignments each day to help someone feel welcomed and valued.

HOME

> Maintain an expectation for godly conversation and actions towards all of God's people when discussing sensitive topics.

> Pray as a family for people in different countries and situations.

> Add a cultural element to your family activities to serve diverse groups and increase awareness.

CHURCH

> Audit current outreach activity and remove or adjust any initiatives that are not having an impact based on feedback from the communities served.

> Proactively build a pipeline of diverse volunteers and partners to work with ministry leaders to ensure good intentions are not misguided by bias or blind spots.

> Invite pastors, ministers, and other faith-based leaders that minister in diverse populations to speak to your leadership team and congregation.

PRAYER

Move Beyond Lip Service
- 1 John 3:17

Heavenly Father, open my eyes to see the needs of people around me. Open my ears to hear their cry. Touch my mind to be moved by compassion toward them. Help me not to shut the door of my heart against them. Instead, let Your love in me lead me to give them from the resources You have blessed me with. Help me to restore their hope again. In Jesus' name, Amen.

Reflection

What specific areas will you pray about from this week's lesson?

❋ _____

❋ _____

❋ _____

❋ _____

❋ _____

What specific actions will you take to move Godward?

❋ _____

❋ _____

❋ _____

❋ _____

❋ _____

Capture your thoughts in the notes section.

Notes

※ _____
※ _____
※ _____
※ _____
※ _____
※ _____
※ _____
※ _____
※ _____
※ _____
※ _____
※ _____
※ _____
※ _____
※ _____
※ _____

WEEK 4:
MAKE ROOM FOR CONTROVERSY AND CONFLICT

QUOTABLES

We must reconcile ourselves to the reality that to follow Jesus means that we, too, must speak out against evil, be hated, be thought demonic, and be polarizing. Any other expectation is wayward."

— Dick Brogden

WEEK 4: MAKE ROOM FOR CONTROVERSY AND CONFLICT

The world is full of sin. This is a result of the fall of man in the Garden of Eden at the beginning of time. Since then, everyone born into this world has the nature of sin and will spend the rest of their life fighting against flesh because sin has been ingrained into our DNA, passed down through our first parents, Adam and Eve. *"Therefore, just as through one man sin entered the world, and death through sin, and thus death spread to all men because all sinned."* (Romans 5:12)

Flesh is the overwhelming desire to sin. For a natural man, it comes easily. One does not have to think twice before one envies a successful person or says some negative things about people. The thought of hurting someone and committing an offense cross people's mind daily. That is how the nature of sin operates. You do not have to force it; it comes naturally, and everybody is guilty of sin. *"If we say that we have not sinned, we make Him a liar, and His word is not in us."* (1 John 1:10)

If sin is a universal experience amongst all and keeps increasing every day, how should we respond as the body of Christ? The simple as is love. Love is the most potent weapon to overcome sin, live a sinless life, and help those struggling get a chance to experience a change of heart

59

and freedom from sin.

God knew the path of man before He created Adam. He knew that man was weak and would struggle with some weaknesses. God understood that man is imperfect and prone to fall. That is why He prepared the way for salvation. *"For God so loved the world that He gave His only begotten Son, that whoever believes in Him should not perish but have everlasting life."* (John 3:16)

The use of words in the Bible is intentional. The Word of God is complete and without any error. What is written there was inspired by God Himself. Therefore, when the Bible says "whoever," means "whoever."

There are no different criteria for salvation based on gender, beliefs, ethnicity, or nationality. God doesn't care about the nature of your sin, whether it is termed great or small, or whether we classify and rank sin based on our own bias towards certain behaviors or lifestyles. Sin is sin, and

the Bible says, *"all have sinned"* (Romans 3:23). Everyone, including believers, is battling sin daily, struggling to subdue it and submit totally to God. Even the apostle Paul admitted his struggle with sin in Romans 7:15-25.

So how should we respond? To answer this critical question, we will consider four examples: three biblical and my personal examples. For the biblical examples, the Prodigal Son, the woman caught in adultery, and the Samaritan Woman will be our case study. These stories show man's imperfect nature and God's unconditional love that superimposes any form of sin, no matter its gravity or nature.

The Prodigal Son (Luke 15:11-32)

The story of the Prodigal Son exemplifies the life of one who was once under God but later went astray. It refers to Christians who left the faith and entered the world to explore and enjoy.

Just as the Prodigal Son took all

his inheritance and left home to squander it on prostitutes and lavish living, we also have taken God's blessings upon our lives for granted, abusing them with a sinful lifestyle.

However, despite the Prodigal Son's disrespect and disregard for his father by demanding his inheritance when he was still alive, his father still cared for him and deeply loved him.

After he had lost all he had to the point of eating with swine, he decided to go back home to seek his father's forgiveness. He knew in his heart that he was not worthy of being called his father's son because of his evil behavior. Therefore, he asked to be considered to become a servant.

However, his father's response when he saw him coming back home was shocking. He rushed down from where he was to meet his sin, who was distant away from the house. He then gave him a tight hug and planted a kiss on his face. Next, he ordered his servants to change his ragged clothes and give him a royal robe, put a ring

on his hand, and sandals on his feet.

His father didn't criticize him or call him names. He didn't say anything about the wayward life he had lived and how he squandered all of his inheritance. Instead, he proved that his son's heart was the most precious thing to him. He loved him, and that was all that mattered.

We learn in this story as believers to be non-judgmental and compassionate. When we come across anyone struggling with sin, we must embrace them with compassion and give them a shoulder to cry on. We must be their safe haven, where they find rest and protection away from the condemnation from the world.

The Woman Caught in Adultery (John 8:1-11)

This remarkable story of a woman caught in adultery shows us people's wicked and hypocritical nature. It demonstrates how people fall into the sin of self-righteousness, neglecting their sins while pointing accusatory fingers at others.

A woman was caught in adultery. The scribes and Pharisees brought her to Jesus and referenced Moses' law, which stipulated that anyone caught in adultery should be stoned. They asked Jesus because they wanted to set a trap for him so they would have a reason to accuse Him based on His position on the matter. If Jesus asked that she should be freed, they would accuse Him of going against the law. And if He agreed and declared she was guilty, then all He had preached about love and forgiveness would mean nothing. This would cause a crack in His ministry, and He would lose His respect and credibility.

But Jesus could see through their scheme. What came out of His mouth was profound. While this lady's accusers were pestering Jesus for His response, He said to them, *"He who is without sin among you, let him throw a stone at her first."* (John 8:7). Pricked by their conscience, they dropped their stones one after the other and left.

When Jesus saw that they had all gone, He said to the accused, *"Woman, where are those accusers of yours? Has no one condemned you?" She said, "No one, Lord."* Then Jesus said He did not condemn her too, and she was free to go and sin no more (John 8:10-12).

Here, Jesus exposes the self-righteousness of man. But beyond that, it illustrates how God's mercy prevails over judgment and how He loves us despite our sins.

The story teaches us to constantly examine our hearts when we find ourselves accusing others of sin because we are also guilty. There is no small or great sin. Sin is sin. Engaging in sin in secret does not make us better than those who openly display their flaws and imperfections.
Like Jesus, we must stop pointing with accusing fingers. We must drop every stone of condemnation. Every moment we see someone falls into sin should

be a time for sober reflection. We must examine our lives and ask serious questions about our standing with God.

God forgives all sins when we repent with sincerity.

The Samaritan Woman (John 4:1-45)

The Samaritan Woman, also known as the woman at the well, suffered heavy discrimination from her community members.

What was her sin? She was married five times and was living with a man she wasn't married to. *"for you have had five husbands, and the one whom you now have is not your husband"* (John 4:18).

Her history of failed relationships became a stigma. People stayed away from their children and warned their children to avoid her because she was seen as a bad example that could negatively influence people to become promiscuous. She was ostracized.

How did we know about her ostracization? The Bible records in John 4:7 that she came to draw water from the well alone. Now, in ancient times, fetching water was an activity that many young ladies looked forward to as it was a period they met in groups to have some girl talk and bond. So, it was always a chore done in a group. However, this was not the case with the Samaritan Woman. She went to the well by herself. Walking or talking with a woman like that could tarnish one's image in society and make one labeled promiscuous. As a result, she was considered a sinner, a cancer cell to be cut off, so it doesn't spread.

But Jesus met her alone at the well and had a deep conversation rich in history and profound spiritual lessons about the living water, spiritual and true worship, and salvation, although He knew about her weakness. Jesus offered Her salvation, and she evangelized Jesus to her community. *"The woman then left her waterpot, went her way into the city, and said to the men, "Come, see a Man who told me*

63

all things that I ever did. Could this be the Christ?" (John 4:28-29)

Most of us are like the Samarians who abandon the weak and wounded instead of offering help and inflict more mental and emotional pain with our words and actions.

On the contrary, Jesus went after the outcast and black sheep among the people. He spent time with them and made them feel seen and loved. He never condemns.

We are called to be like Jesus, not running from people different from us but making room for controversy and conflict so we can connect as humans without the religious veil that has blinded us and made us turn against each other.

MY STORY

My son came out as queer after graduating from college. There was chaos swirling around me from gossiping family, friends, and fellow believers. Everyone had an opinion about what I should do. Christian counsel offered generic advice like praying and trusting God. While the situation was overwhelming, I was not confused about how to respond to my son when he came out. I reassured him that I would always love him. I spoke to him as I always had about God having a plan for his life and that he is created to be a mighty man of valor. I will always pray for him and call forth the God-given greatness in him until God calls me home.

My love response for my son did not go over well with my zealous family and friends. I remember thinking, "Do these people really believe I should turn my back on my son? I'd die for him." And quite frankly, anyone who ever bothered my son would be in for some pretty severe consequences from me. That's the most Christian way my southern-born and raised self can express my response to anyone that dared to mess with my precious first-born child.

I also said to myself, I've prayed

with some of these people when their daughters became pregnant out of wedlock, their sons were admitted to rehab or incarcerated, their spouses had affairs, and more. Now they want to shun me and tell me to turn on my son. Really?

And here is a great controversy. How should we respond to the issues that so many place at the top of their list of sins?

While I have more questions than answers relative to these complex issues, I sincerely believe, based on Christ's examples, the answer is love. And putting it frankly, "The same way you want Christ to respond to the sin in your life."

This ongoing reality is one of the many reasons I refuse to check a box. I will never compromise my faith in my son, popular thinking, or a political agenda. And I will never turn my back on my son for friends, family, a political agenda, or a false narrative of force-ranked sin.

Practical ways to respond to controversial situations and conflicts as a believer.

ALWAYS TRY TO CALL PEOPLE IN.

Never call people out. Call out specific behaviors and address them accordingly but always try to call the person into fellowship with other believers and a relationship with Jesus Christ. Pray about what to say or do in touchy situations. By all means, do not drag people out in the open, pointing accusing fingers at them while trying to stone them.

LOOK DEEP WITHIN

Look inward. Check yourself thoroughly. And ask yourself, are you perfect? Consider the gravity of your past and secret sins and how God has been merciful. Then extend the mercy you have received to the person overwhelmed by weaknesses and flaws.

WHAT WOULD JESUS DO?

This is a simple but profound question to always ask yourself when confronted with controversy and conflict. What would Jesus do if He encounters a Prodigal Son, the adulterous woman, a Samaritan woman, or my son? Would He judge and banish them to hell or pray and bless them? Would Jesus crucify them or sacrifice Himself for them? Would He chase them away or offer them a shoulder? Think about these, search the scriptures for answers, then practice what you discover.

What visual of DEI do you want people and the body of Christ to aspire to?

Consider Jesus's disciples. Jesus chose to closely associate with people from all walks of life. Many times, He interacted with people that "the church" shunned.

The good Samaritan offers a great example as well. The Bible provides model examples of diversity, equity, and inclusion.

What are yours? We can't go wrong when we treat people the way God invites us to in the Bible.

Assessment

I say no to requests that marginalize or exclude others. _____

I remain open to the possibility that someone else's lived experience may differ significantly from mine. And just because something is not happening to me doesn't mean it's not happening. _____

I advocate for following Christ's example of inclusion in complicated and polarizing situations. _____

I apply a lens of truth when evaluating information, including scripture, Godly counsel, and evidence-based data. _____

I speak up with love when confronted with exclusionary behavior and ungodly comments. _____

What are your areas of strength? How have they shown up in your life?

※ _____

※ _____

What are your areas of opportunity? How have they shown up in your life?

※ _____

※ _____

APPLICATION

SELF

> Identify how bias may unknowingly influence your decision-making.

> Develop conscious choices to mitigate biased behavior.

> Practice the PAUSE process when dealing with conflict.

HOME

> Call out and address microaggressions and discrimination and encourage your family and friends to do the same.

> Select someone with very different views from you to serve as a sounding board for ideas related to DEI.

> Practice the PAUSE process when people are upset or unsure about how to handle differences of opinion.

CHURCH

> If they don't already exist, establish ministry safe spaces that mitigate church politics and allow people to share their experiences, and openly discuss where they are when it comes to DEI—all with the goal of moving toward God's model for inclusion.

> Include segments on polarizing events and topics in bible study and teaching to avoid popular thinking that contradicts sound biblical principles.

PRAYER

Make Room for Controversy and Conflict
- 1 John 3:18

Great God, I ask for the capacity to love everyone I come across through my actions and not words alone. Help me to commit to acts of kindness and goodness. Let everyone who encounters me be blessed by good deeds and experience Your love through me. Help me to understand that love is an action word that must be demonstrated deliberately to the marginalized, oppressed and abandoned. In Jesus' name, Amen.

Reflection

What specific areas will you pray about from this week's lesson?

※ _____

※ _____

※ _____

※ _____

※ _____

What specific actions will you take to move Godward?

※ _____

※ _____

※ _____

※ _____

※ _____

Capture your thoughts in the notes section.

Notes

❈ _____

❈ _____

❈ _____

❈ _____

❈ _____

❈ _____

❈ _____

❈ _____

❈ _____

❈ _____

❈ _____

❈ _____

❈ _____

❈ _____

❈ _____

❈ _____

WEEK 5:
INVITE NEW
PERSPECTIVES

QUOTABLES

I like to say I'm not a Republican or a Democrat, I'm a Christ-o-crat.

— Rod Parsley

WEEK 5: INVITE NEW PERSPECTIVES

Diversity is God's best gift to humanity. Imagine a world where everything and everyone is similar. A generic world where we all speak the same language, dress the same way, have the same heritage and belief system, etc. The world would lose its savor and beauty. It would become uninteresting and predictable.

Our minds would become shallow and unstimulated. We would lose our creative juice and critical thinking sense and begin to experience a decline in intellectual capacity and life in general.

In a nutshell, if we do not learn, we die. To learn, there must be new knowledge and challenging and unfamiliar ideas that will trigger our critical thinking faculty and help our minds to wander and seek answers. We must understand that we must engage with new ideas and perspectives with an open mind to grow and expand in every area of our lives.

For light to be relevant, there must be darkness. The sun would lose its relevance and become a source of pain to us if there wasn't the moon to govern the night. The blue and clear sky would become boring without a dark sky displaying the flickering stars.

In other words, the same perspective and linear life is boring. Life makes sense when there are diversions, roadblocks, bumps, and sometimes accidents. That is what makes it adventurous and meaningful. This is why God's creative diversity is the spice of life and the paints on a blank canvas called life. It gives flavor to life's blandness and color to its dullness.

This should be your perspective when dealing with different people, traditions, ways of life, and thinking. You must not run away from the unfamiliar but embrace it as a gift handed to you by God for you to grow, break away from the box limiting you, and experience life in a new dimension.

God understood the value of diversity, which is why He created a man and a woman during creation and blessed them with different minds and bodies that function differently. God knew the level of exploit they would do and the tremendous thing they would achieve if they remained united in purpose while embracing their differences simultaneously (Genesis 1:28).

Therefore, you must begin to work on your mind to see newness not as a threat but as an opportunity to elevate from a lower level of awareness to a higher one. You must be humble to know that every individual bears a gift that can improve your life and make you experience life in a new way.

However, inviting new perspectives might be challenging, primarily if you have held on to your one-sided view of life and heard and believed a one-sided story that has become a significant part of your thinking process and perception of life.

So, what do you do?

LEAD WITH CURIOSITY

Curiosity is a blessing. It is through being curious that we discover new ideas and knowledge.

God's Word encourages curiosity. *"Ask, and it will be given to you; seek, and you will find; knock, and it will be opened to you. For everyone who asks receives, and he who seeks finds, and to him who knocks, it will be opened."* (Matthew 7:7-8).

This powerful scripture shows the benefits of curiosity. Curiosity opens doors to new discoveries about people and how things work. It answers the questions of life and reveals uncommon truths.

You must understand that you can learn something from everyone you meet, irrespective of how much you think you know. One formidable enemy that has defeated many people is the know-it-all mentality. It has robbed many of opportunities and made them stagnant.

Once growth stops, decline and death are inevitable. Therefore, you must remove the garment of pride and the badge of arrogance on your chest and choose humility.

Be curious about how people think, why they act the way they do and why they make certain choices and decisions. Be slow to criticize. Avoid the cancel culture by all means and offer people the chance to voice their minds. By doing these, you give your mind permission to explore and learn. Most importantly, you give someone a chance to speak.

Many people's voices have been suppressed for so long.

They have been shoved to the side and treated like they do not matter. They yearn for a platform to amplify their voice and make them heard. It would mean so much to them. Why not be the one who fulfills this passionate dream?

Entertaining new perspectives is a double-edged sword. It sharpens your mind and fulfills the dream of another. Therefore, lead with curiosity.

RECOGNIZE AND RESPECT THE INHERENT VALUE IN EVERY PERSON.

One quality that sets Jesus apart is His respect for every person. He was accessible to all and mingled with people from different walks of life, backgrounds, and orientations. Jesus never despised anyone but mostly had deep conversations with them to understand their thoughts. No wonder it was easy for Him to convince them about His mission and God's Kingdom and win their hearts.

Jesus looked beyond people's stereotypes and limitations and negativity blocking their minds. That was why He rebuked His disciples when they complained when a woman anointed Him with an alabaster flask of very expensive ointment (Matthew 26:6-13). While His disciples saw a waste of money, Jesus saw immense value in her act as she was preparing Him for one of the greatest parts of His ministry and salvation plan for humanity; His death.

We should treat anyone you meet as a treasure box with valuables that can give you great fortune now or in the future. Remember the leprous warrior who rose to the rank of commander of the army of the king of Aram, Naaman? (2 Kings 5) He had everything but suffered leprosy. But the information that led to his healing came from the most unlikely person, his wife's servant girl.

Imagine if Naaman was not open to new perspectives and disdained the girl's advice to go to Israel and meet the prophet Elisha for healing. He would have died a leper.

We learn from this story that everyone is valuable and their knowledge and idea matter. You might be surprised that the person holding the key to your open door might just be a struggling immigrant who does menial jobs to fend for himself.

Try to see people as souls that can be won to the kingdom of God, especially when we disagree. Disagreement is an opportunity to learn and teach, not a time to demean and block your mind and resist new ideas because you're comfortable with them.

THE ROLE OF THE FAITH COMMUNITY

In my book, You're Still Good; I shared my testimony of God's miraculous healing power. My daughter suffered a stroke at the age of 17. I've noticed several recurring questions each time I share with a new group.

Why did you drive your daughter to the hospital instead of calling 911? In public, I usually respond by saying I knew I needed to get her to the hospital as quickly as possible, which is true. I'm sharing the deeper truth behind my actions with you.

There is a sentiment among the Black community that 911 response times are slower in predominately Black lower-income neighborhoods. I'd heard this repeated throughout my entire life, including in the church.

I've also heard, read, and been told that Black women are much more likely to be underdiagnosed and not treated for serious acute illnesses. So when I got to the hospital with my daughter and the nurse kept telling me to have a seat, I was utterly triggered because I knew from my own medical training and my pure mother instinct that something was seriously wrong with my daughter.

I really had to fight to get them to give her urgent care. "This is my daughter, and I know something serious is going on!" I insisted. A nurse finally checked Jasmine's blood pressure, and it was like all the blood rushed out of her face. She ran to call a code that made other nurses and doctors come running. By this time, Jasmine was completely non-responsive. They put her on an IV, and once she was stabilized, they took her for a CAT scan. She had a massive blood clot and also a bleed in her brain.

After the doctors delivered the poor prognosis, they sent the hospital chaplain in to ask me if I needed anything. I promptly responded, "Yes, can you print me out some healing scriptures?" The look of bewilderment on the Chaplain's face still baffles me. As followers of Jesus Christ, we have an opportunity to share hope and faith in times of despair. In fairness, I guess he did not want to get my hopes up, seeing that the doctors all but said my daughter was going to die.

Now let's parse this out a bit. What if the intake nurse had invited a new perspective on why some Black people and communities of color tend to bring their loved ones to the hospital instead of calling 911? Could she have done a better job triaging our emergency? Could she have avoided her false assumption that someone who walks into the hospital or is wheeled in by a family member is not to automatically be considered as being in less critical condition?

A couple of the other frequent questions from people familiar with my testimony are: Why did you ask the Chaplain for healing scriptures? My question is, why was the Chaplain of all people so taken aback when I asked him to print some healing scriptures? Another question is," Weren't you afraid of being labeled a fanatic when you prayed in tongues in front of medical staff?" My faith is not something I do on Sundays; it's who I am—the very essence of my being.

After repeatedly hearing these types of questions, I realized the situation with my daughter offered some great teachable moments to invite new perspectives. I offered some evidence-based data on EMT response times from an article titled "Study Shows EMS Response Times Are Slower in Low-Income Areas" by EMS World News to help medical workers and others understand what people sometimes label as perceptions in people with different backgrounds and experiences is actually steeped reality.

According to the article, "A nationwide study of more than 63,000 cases of cardiac arrest found that ambulances on average took nearly four minutes longer to handle calls from low-income areas than high-income communities."

I also designed an application bible study for believers to work through challenges when facing tragic events. It's available for anyone to download on my website. lawanaharris.com

I share this story specifically because I consider the church to be a hospital of sorts. People come to church broken, hurt, battered, and bruised. They may show up just after a domestic dispute, a painful divorce, or after being released from rehab or prison.

Are you part of a "come as you are" church or a "get in where you fit in" church? We have an awesome opportunity and responsibility to shepherd and disciple the people that come to our ministry. How can we be sure that our faith community is a safe and welcoming place for everyone?

❋ _____

❋ _____

Are we worshiping in a bubble?

❋ _____

❋ _____

How can we open ourselves up to better understand the people we are called to serve?

❋ _____

❋ _____

The church must not be blinded and limited by human doctrines and traditions. Instead, we must follow God's way when dealing with the hurt and wounded. We must apply the divine principle Jesus used that brought healing and salvation to all - love. We must accept everyone in love as they are. We must respond to their needs with urgency, treating their wounds and walking them through their healing journey until they are filled with the love of Jesus that transforms.

Assessment

I help create an environment where others can come as they are to establish a relationship with Jesus Christ. _____

I approach conflict with humility and vulnerability and remain open to new information and insights from the Holy Spirit. _____

I invite opposing thoughts and ideas when making decisions to understand additional perspectives. _____

I invite the Lord to order my steps in any direction he chooses according to his sovereign will. _____

I pray for guidance and discernment relative to any unintended consequences when engaging in ministry with people from different backgrounds and cultures. _____

What are your areas of strength? How have they shown up in your life?

※ _____

※ _____

What are your areas of opportunity? How have they shown up in your life?

※ _____

※ _____

APPLICATION

SELF

> Proactively seek feedback from fellow believers who are different from you to understand the reality others face on a daily basis.

> Reflect on your "fellowship circles." Be aware of stereotypes creeping into your thinking and actions.

> Participate in virtual prayer groups and bible study groups to fellowship with a diverse mix of believers.

HOME

> Have an open discussion about how you and others were raised and how your upbringing aligns with Christ's teachings.

> Pray about any areas in current times or from past experiences that are not in line with how Jesus related to people with different beliefs, values and backgrounds.

> Create an "oral tradition" by inviting family and friends to share their "How I was raised" stories. Discuss and celebrate the differences.

CHURCH

> Get out into communities and serve! Suspend all judgment and love on people.

> Host "Faith-based Inclusion" meetings with international ministry partners and ensure a diversity of voices are represented in your annual planning calendar.

> Bring the outside in by collaborating with external partners to share biblical perspectives that may be underrepresented in your congregation during special services and celebrations.

PRAYER

Invite New Perspectives
- Romans 2:11

Lord Jesus, Your Word says there's no partiality with You. Therefore, I ask for the grace to embrace diversity, equity, and inclusion. Help me to consider people's humanness above their race, gender, religion, and sexual orientation. Teach me to see Your beauty and gifts in people's lives while also appreciating the differences associated with nationality, socioeconomic status, language, disability, and age. In Jesus' name, Amen.

Reflection

What specific areas will you pray about from this week's lesson?

❈ _____

❈ _____

❈ _____

❈ _____

❈ _____

What specific actions will you take to move Godward?

❈ _____

❈ _____

❈ _____

❈ _____

❈ _____

Capture your thoughts in the notes section.

84

Notes

�֍ _____

✖ _____

✖ _____

✖ _____

✖ _____

✖ _____

✖ _____

✖ _____

✖ _____

✖ _____

✖ _____

✖ _____

✖ _____

✖ _____

✖ _____

WEEK 6:
TELL THE TRUTH
EVEN WHEN
IT HURTS

QUOTABLES

"You are part and parcel of this nation, for you share in its protection and privileges, and it is yours as Christian men to feel that you are bound in return to do all you can to promote truth and righteousness."

— Charles Spurgeon

WEEK 6: TELL THE TRUTH EVEN WHEN IT HURTS

Jesus Christ speaking in John 8:32, says, *"And you shall know the truth, and the truth shall make you free."* This statement reveals the power of truth. The truth enlightens and brings us out from the dark pit of ignorance into a place of knowledge and awareness. It also breaks us free from the shackles of ignorance. When these two things happen, you become empowered. Because when you know better, you do better. Ignorance is not a curse but an opportunity to learn and grow. It is when we refuse to pursue the truth to elevate above clueless to understanding that there's a problem.

However, just as the truth brings light and freedom, it can also inflict deep painful cuts into our ego and belief systems. The truth is sharp and a bitter pill to swallow, especially when it challenges what we have become familiar with and comfortable around. But the truth cannot be covered or hidden; it always reveals itself. It must be said, even if it hurts.

Churches, mission teams, outreach groups, and volunteers have played active roles in ministering in diverse communities and countries ravaged by poverty and economic hardship, war, natural disasters, health issues, and other crises.

These groups of people have done exceptionally well in catering to people's needs, cushioning the effects of problems, and championing the cause of diversity, equity and inclusion. They try to create opportunities and an enabling environment for these communities to thrive and live their best lives. However, sometimes, we innocently and unknowingly create other problems with our good deeds.

Churches, mission teams, and outreach groups inadvertently cause harm even with the best intentions when ministering in diverse communities and countries. That is the truth we often want to shy away from, but the evidence is there.

Looking deeper at a couple ministry examples, there were separate events that took place on two mission trips but shared the same erroneous thinking. I was with a local mission team in the projects. Some of the team members were engaged in children's ministry and games. I was assigned to the food distribution team on that day. I noticed some fruits and vegetables were withered and starting to grow mold. I mentioned the condition of the fresh foods to the team captain, who responded, "Don't worry about it. They should be happy to get anything we bring."

A similar situation took place in Haiti during a clothes distribution. I was sorting through the donations and removing the worn or soiled items. One of the other members of the team approached me and said, "Look around; they will be glad to get anything we give them."

How, then, can we say we are championing diversity, equity, and inclusion when we still belittle people and feel we are superior to them? How can we have the mindset that they deserve nothing but crumbs, leftovers, and waste as food and rags as clothing because they do not have options?

It is quite unfortunate that we have weaponized their desperation for survival against them and used it to subject them to unfair treatment, thereby making us the same monsters we are fighting.

This trend is noticeable everywhere, even in the corporate world, where we save the best jobs for the privileged and "our people" even when they are underqualified but subject immigrants to domestic and menial jobs and paid peanuts because we are aware they have limited options. While those who are lucky to gain employment in an ideal organization are given lower pay than their colleagues at similar positions even when they qualify for more and are not promoted because "they will be glad to get anything we give them."

So-called "mission work" has become an avenue for people to pursue their personal interests and not that of the locals. Many rich 'volunteers' join churches and outreach groups that travel to Africa, and other developing nations only to feel good about saving the world and creating positive change. Still, these countries never get the assistance they need and continue to suffer impoverished conditions.

Is this what God wants? Is this how He responds to us when we are in distress? From a spiritual point of view, we were not different from communities and people suffering prejudice and discrimination. We were once subjected to this same experience at the hand of the devil because of our sins. We suffered constant harassment from evil spirits and were cut off from spiritual opportunities and blessings.

However, when it was time for God to intervene and deliver humanity from troubles, He sent His only Son, Jesus Christ. God did not send an angel or one of the twenty-four elders. He sent His one and only beloved Son. He gave the world His best to deliver us from destruction and reconcile us back to Him so that we would become free from spiritual oppression and joint heirs with Christ (equity), having access to heavenly blessings and privileges.

That is what we should do for others that need our help. We must be compassionate and generous at the same time. We cannot claim to love people and mistreat them. We must approach this group of people with the attitude that whatever we do for them, we do it for the Lord. Jesus says in Matthew 25:35-40:

"For I was hungry and you gave Me food; I was thirsty and you gave Me drink; I was a stranger and you took Me in; I was naked and you clothed Me; I was sick and you visited Me; I was in prison and you came to Me.' "Then the righteous will answer Him, saying, 'Lord, when did we see You hungry and feed You, or thirsty and give You drink? When did we see You a stranger and take You in, or naked and clothe You? Or when did we see You sick, or in prison, and come to You?' And the King will answer and say to them, 'Assuredly, I say to you, inasmuch as you did it to one of the least of these My brethren, you did it to Me."

The story of Cain and Abel comes to mind here. What is the state of your heart when you give? Do you give with the right attitude or for some selfish reasons? God does not care about the many activities we organize to drive diversity, equity, and inclusion. He wants to know the motivation behind all that we do. God rejected Cain's sacrifice but accepted Abel's own because His heart was right with God. *"By faith Abel offered to God a more excellent sacrifice than Cain, through which he obtained witness that he was righteous, God testifying of his gift."* (Hebrews 11:4)

THE WAY FORWARD.

DO SOME HEART WORK

We must work on our minds and intentions if we do not want God to reject our labor in ensuring diversity, equity, and inclusion. We must always see others as God's image and treat them as we would treat God. We must determine in our hearts to give them the best or nothing and purge our hearts of every ulterior motive and personal agenda. Once the purpose of our mission is clear, and our hearts are pure, giving our best to help people would become easy and rewarding. You will feel true satisfaction in yourself, and the Lord will be pleased with you.

Allow love to find a place in your heart. Love makes it easy to serve others. Love can also fix your heart if you struggle with doing what is right.

Let God fill your heart with love and transform your stony heart into the heart of flesh. *"And though I bestow all my goods to feed the poor, and though I give my body to be burned, but have not love, it profits me nothing."* (1 Corinthians 13:3)

BE SELFLESS

Selfless is putting others' needs ahead of yours. The Bible says, "Let no one seek his own, but each one the other's well-being." (1 Corinthians 10:24). One truth about mission work is that many people do it for their personal gain and glory, not for the marginalized, not for God's glory. While some people do it to brag about their humanitarian services in a war-torn country or poverty-stricken nations, others do it for the pictures and life-affirming experience.

We can't afford to toy with people's life and existence because of mundane things. We must prioritize their needs with urgency and the understanding that their lives and destinies depend on it. We should help them without expecting any form of reward. We must consider it a service to God.

"Finally, all of you be of one mind, having compassion for one another; love as brothers, be tenderhearted, be courteous" (1 Peter 3:8)

FIRST DO NO HARM

Ideas like voluntourism, where people pay to visit orphanages and do some humanitarian services in developing nations, have attracted the world's attention negatively. Many people now see that voluntourism does not solve the problems of these communities but leaves them as they are or compound them. Thousands of dollars are spent on organizing trips, rescuing children and taking them to orphanages, buying food items and other relief materials, and building schools and wells. This type of humanitarian aid and missionary work is a blessing in most cases.

Unfortunately, some of these materials and monies are frequently mismanaged by corrupt politicians, customs agents and local leaders. The children still remain impoverished and are purposely kept in a deplorable condition so more money could flow in.

Now that this truth is known, we have a responsibility to be diligent stewards with our money and resources. That said, this dynamic creates a difficult situation to serve people with excellence while avoiding being scammed by ruthless, greedy opportunists.

Some people have vowed not to donate to charity organizations anymore because of the mismanagement of funds.

What can the church do to mitigate this problem?

❋ _____

❋ _____

What can be done to win back people's trust and restore their confidence in giving and helping?
Going through well-established organizations to reach out to people is good start and the church should connect to the needy directly as we work to restores people's trust to donate.

❋ _____

❋ _____

The church must also emphasize that God rewards all our service done with the right motive, including taking a stand for diversity, equity, and inclusion at home and abroad. Proverbs 19:17 says, "The one who is gracious to the poor lends to the LORD, and the LORD will repay him for his good deed."

Assessment

I recognize that there are some good, bad and ugly aspects of history that impact our lives today. _____

I speak the truth about Christ's examples for DEI even when it may not be well received. _____

I consistently honor my faith, my values, and my beliefs when faced with complex or sensitive topics. _____

I speak the truth in love even when I strongly disagree with someone. _____

I "walk the talk" of inclusion by treating everyone with dignity and respect without judgment. _____

What are your areas of strength? How have they shown up in your life?

❈ _____

❈ _____

What are your areas of opportunity? How have they shown up in your life?

❈ _____

❈ _____

APPLICATION

SELF

> Ask God to show you any area of your heart that he wants to heal and restore based on past hurts.

> Develop prayer and meditation practices such as journaling and physical activity to remain peaceful when current events test your faith.

> Take a hard look at the "why" behind your reasons for and against certain DEI-related issues. Is the "why" grounded in biblical principles or popular opinion?

HOME

> Ask the Holy Spirit to lead and guide you into all truth as promised in John 16:13.

> Establish ground rules for family and friend interactions around polarizing topics. Create honest conversations without judgment or damaging family relationships. Agree to stop the conversation if it looks like it will interfere with your ability to fellowship with one another.

CHURCH

> Share relevant scripture, articles, books, and TED talks that demonstrate linkages between your local teaching, bible study, and sermons.

> Partner with external associations serving diverse demographics to get started if you have not served in those areas before.

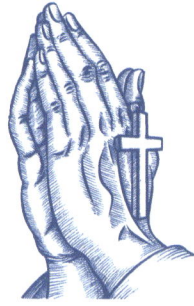

PRAYER

Tell the Truth Even When it Hurts
- Revelation 7:9

Mighty God, I ask for the boldness to stand for the truth even when I am the only one standing. Help me to tell the truth even when my voice is the lowest. Give me the courage to remain steadfast even amidst opposition and criticism. Let my determination influence others to recognize and accept the truth and live by it. In Jesus' name, Amen.

Reflection

What specific areas will you pray about from this week's lesson?

- ※ ______________________________
- ※ ______________________________
- ※ ______________________________
- ※ ______________________________
- ※ ______________________________

What specific actions will you take to move Godward?

- ※ ______________________________
- ※ ______________________________
- ※ ______________________________
- ※ ______________________________
- ※ ______________________________

Capture your thoughts in the notes section.

Notes

❈ _____

❈ _____

❈ _____

❈ _____

❈ _____

❈ _____

❈ _____

❈ _____

❈ _____

❈ _____

❈ _____

❈ _____

❈ _____

❈ _____

❈ _____

❈ _____

THE FUEL:
THE FRUIT OF
THE SPIRIT

THE FUEL: THE FRUIT OF THE SPIRIT

Galations 5:22 says, "But the fruit of the Spirit is love, joy, peace, patience, kindness, goodness, faithfulness, gentleness, and self-control. Against such things there is no law."

A biblical way of saying, "take action" is "bear fruit." The fruit of the spirit refers both to a way of being, and a way of action. Love is a noun, but it is also a verb. We are called to be loving, and to love others. Let's consider the other "fruits of the Spirit" as they pertain to ways of both acting and being, and let's apply it specifically to God's heart for diversity, equity, and inclusion. Now let's explore the Fruit of the Spirit as practical principles to put our commitment into action to be salt and light to this generation.

WEEK 7:
LOVE:
THE TRUE LOVE
OUR WORLD
NEEDS

QUOTABLES

"Jesus didn't wait until we got better to die for us. He died when we were in our most unlovely state. The person who doesn't deserve love actually needs love more, not less. If you know someone unworthy of love, that's great! You now have a chance to emulate Christ, because the essence of His love is unconditional."

— Tony Evans

WEEK 7 LOVE: THE TRUE LOVE OUR WORLD NEEDS

Think back on the past week. How many times did you think or say, *"I LOVE this..."*? Maybe you love your morning cup of coffee, the way the birds sing outside your window, or how excited your pet gets when they know it's time to go for a walk.

If you're like others, it may be that last tick of the workday clock. Or that new gadget or gadget upgrade you just got. As human beings, it's easy to see the things we love and be passionate about them. After all, when we feel that moment of joy, it's hard to resist expressing those emotions.

And maybe, love looks like the smile of a child. The touch of a spouse. A hug from a friend. The kindness of a stranger in an unexpected place.

When we consider the love that God speaks of in the Bible, it's more than just a feeling or emotion. It's an action and a choice to show kindness, compassion, acceptance, patience, understanding, and grace. Love is not something you can buy; it's something you give away freely with no strings attached.

Love is a powerful thing. It drives us to do extraordinary things in the face of adversity. It motivates us to go beyond our boundaries and take risks for a better future. It can even cause us to act against our own self-interests in order to do good.

However, love can often lose its focus in the hustle and bustle of everyday life. We can become complacent, jaded, or even cynical. Think about it - how often do we throw the word "love" around on things that aren't that important in the grand scheme of life?

In Galatians 5:22-23 (NIV), Paul wrote of the fruit of the Holy Spirit. He said, "But the fruit of the Spirit is love, joy, peace, forbearance, kindness, goodness, faithfulness, gentleness, and self-control." Listed at the first of the fruits of Spirit is "Love."

Paul's original readers may have lived in a different time than us, but they were humans all the same. They knew that love was essential to living in harmony with ourselves, each other, and God. And - just like we do - they often struggled to keep those moments of love at the forefront of everyday life.

The Bible is our north star when it comes to the concept and practice of Love. 1 John 4:7-11 (NIV) says, "Beloved, let us love one another, for love is from God; and everyone who loves is born of God and knows God. The one who does not love does not know God, for God is love."

The original language of the Bible carries the message a bit further. The words of 1 John 4:7-11 (NIV) use the Greek word "agape," - which is an unconditional love that embraces even people who are different than us. This type of love, in theory, requires us to think beyond our own needs and wants. It extends an embrace to those who are different than us, offering understanding and respect. It is different from the other uses of love in the Bible, such as "phileo," which is a more familiar type of love, and "eros," which is passionate or romantic.

It's this "agape" love that Paul is referring to when he lists "Love" as the first of the fruits of Spirit. It's an active and intentional showing of kindness, respect, and understanding that we are called to practice with everyone around us, regardless of who they are or their beliefs.

You may have heard of this

love expressed at a wedding. 1 Corinthians 13 is a popular passage that speaks about this agape love:

"Love is patient, love is kind. It does not envy, it does not boast, it is not proud. It does not dishonor others, it is not self-seeking, it is not easily angered, it keeps no record of wrongs. Love does not delight in evil but rejoices with the truth. It always protects, always trusts, always hopes, always perseveres."

This definition of love is directed at marriage - but it can go so much further. And in a world that has lost its way, this type of love is needed more than ever. It's a way to bring people together and find common ground - even in the midst of disagreement. It forces us to see the other person as someone created in the image of God and worthy of our respect. It's a way to bridge divides and foster understanding - without compromising our own beliefs or values.

Jesus Christ showed us the way - through His example of agape love. He didn't shy away from tough conversations; instead, He embraced them with grace and humility that is hard to come by. Likewise, we can strive to do the same - not just in our own lives but also in our churches and beyond.

And when it came time to choose His followers, He didn't just pick the ones who agreed with Him; He chose the most unlikely of candidates - tax collectors and prostitutes. Those who had been rejected by society and left behind. He welcomed them with open arms, loving and accepting each one as if they were His own family.

Jesus has loved each of us, even at the cost of His own life. And when we know that depth of love, it's easy to carry that same type of love and compassion into our own lives. So the next time you reach for "love" in your daily life, think to yourself - how can I practice the agape love of Christ today? If God loved us enough to die for us, surely we can love each other enough to live in harmony with one another!

SCRIPTURES TO MEDITATE ON

John 15:12-13 (NIV)- "My command is this: Love each other as I have loved you. Greater love has no one than this: to lay down one's life for one's friends.

❋ _____

❋ _____

1 Corinthians 13:4-8 (NIV) - "Love is patient, love is kind. It does not envy, it does not boast, it is not proud. It does not dishonor others, it is not self-seeking, it is not easily angered, it keeps no record of wrongs."

❋ _____

❋ _____

1 John 4:7-11 (NIV): "Dear friends, let us love one another, for love comes from God. Everyone who loves has been born of God and knows God. Whoever does not love does not know God, because God is love."

❋ _____

❋ _____

John 3:16 (NIV): "For God so loved the world that he gave his one and only Son, that whoever believes in him shall not perish but have eternal life."

❋ _____

❋ _____

5 STATEMENTS TO MEASURE THE FRUIT OF JOY

❈ I will redefine love based on the agape love shown by Jesus.

❈ I will actively seek to understand others and bridge divides with love.

❈ I will practice the same grace, humility, and acceptance that Jesus did.

❈ I will strive to show kindness and respect to all people, even those who disagree with me.

❈ I will do my best to view everyone as created in the image of the Creator who designed love.

REFLECTION QUESTIONS

1. How have you seen Jesus' love manifested in your life? In people? At particular places?

❈ _____

❈ _____

2. What are some practical ways that you can practice agape love towards others?

❈ _____

❈ _____

3. How has the concept of "love" been defined for you in the past, and how will you redefine it today?

❈ _____

❈ _____

4. Are there any people or situations in your life where you are having difficulty showing love? How can you adjust your perspective to foster a better understanding?

❋ _____

❋ _____

How to Increase Love in...

MYSELF

Cultivating love within ourselves is essential if we are to show it to others. We can start by deepening our relationship with God, reading His Word regularly, and submitting ourselves to Him daily. We take hope in the truth of the Bible: that God loves us unconditionally and wants to be in a relationship with us.

When we understand this truth, it's easier to love ourselves and others. We can also practice self-care and take time for rest, relaxation, and prayer. These things will help us stay grounded in a loving mindset - one that looks to serve others without any expectation of return.

Our world is so full of misplaced definitions of "love," and the only way to combat this is to start by loving ourselves. When we accept God's love for us, it spreads outward in a beautiful wave of compassion and understanding. Run to the loving arms of the Father, and let His grace fill your being!

YOUR CHURCH

The church is the perfect place to foster understanding and love for one another, no matter our differences in race, gender, socioeconomic status, or beliefs. We can start by displaying respect for each other's opinions and points of view - even if we don't agree.

We can also look for ways to bridge the divides between various groups within the church. This could be as simple as hosting a monthly potluck meal or gathering friends from different backgrounds together for an activity that brings joy and unity. We should also strive to ensure our church is meeting the needs of all its members, regardless of their situation or background.

Finally, we can be intentional about creating a safe space for conversations that may be uncomfortable but are necessary to fostering true love and understanding in our church. When everyone feels like their opinion is respected and valued, we create an atmosphere of genuine care and acceptance - something God desires for His Church!

THE WORLD

It's all too easy to get caught up in our everyday lives and forget that we're called to love people even outside of our comfort zones. We can start by seeking out opportunities to serve or help others, regardless of their background or beliefs. From volunteering at a local soup kitchen to showing kindness to strangers on the street, these little acts of love can make a big difference.

We also need to be mindful of the power of our words and actions - both online and off. With so much divisiveness in our world today, it's essential that we choose to speak and act with kindness and understanding. We should strive to listen more than we talk, recognize people's lived experiences, and keep an open mind as we learn from one another.

Finally, prayer is the greatest way to spread love throughout our world. Pray for peace, healing, and reconciliation - that God's love would be made known in all places. Ask Him to show you how He wants to use you in this mission to bridge divides and bring light to dark places. When we start our mission of love on our knees, we will soon see that love overflowing into our world!

109

PRAYER

Dear Heavenly Father, thank You for Your unconditional love and grace. We know that this is the foundation for all other kinds of love - even when it feels impossible to give or receive. Help us to remember this truth as we strive to be vessels of Your love in our lives, church, and world. We pray for hearts that are open to understanding and acceptance of one another. Send us out each day with boldness to share the light of Your love! In Jesus' Name, Amen.

WEEK 8:
JOY: FINDING AND SPREADING JOY IN OUR LIVES

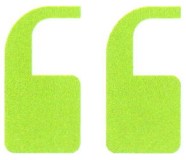

QUOTABLES

Remember that we know how the story ends…and it is a happy, happy ending!

— Marilyn Hickey

WEEK 8: JOY: FINDING AND SPREADING JOY IN OUR LIVES

Here's a simple question that may not be that easy to answer: *What brings you joy? When you find it, what does it look like?*

We all have different ideas about what joy looks like and how to get there, but the Bible tells us that Joy is a fruit of the Spirit!

For some, it may be spending time with family and friends; for others, it might be enjoying a good book or visiting a new place. Others may find joy in volunteering or making a difference in the world. Of course, we all have different sources of joy, but knowing how to identify and nurture it is integral to living a whole and meaningful life.

This is especially true when it comes to the fruit of the spirit, joy. The Bible says in Galatians 5:22-23 that "the fruit of the Spirit is love, joy, peace, patience, kindness, goodness, faithfulness, gentleness, and self-control." All of these are essential qualities that should be cultivated in our lives, but joy is especially meaningful.

Joy is not just a feeling; it's a way of looking at the world and finding purpose in life. It's more than simply having a moment of happiness; it's about having a long-term outlook of hope and optimism. When joy fills our souls, even the toughest of times can become bearable, and we can have faith that God will provide us with the strength we need to get through it.

Yet it's not hard to look around and see that our world is often filled with sadness and despair. We are surrounded by people who are struggling, and it can be easy to forget about joy in the face of so much pain. Perhaps that is why the Apostle Paul placed this fruit of the Spirit so highly, reminding us that joy is essential to living a life of faith.

Paul sprinkles calls to joy throughout his letters in the New Testament. In Philippians 4:4, "Rejoice in the Lord always. I will say it again: Rejoice!" He's telling us to look for joy in our lives and be thankful for it. We can take this to heart and use it as a reminder that no matter what is happening in the world, we can find joy if we open ourselves up to it.

Jesus, Himself said in John 15:11, "These things I have spoken to you, that My joy may remain in you, and that your joy may be full." Jesus' joy was overflowing and contagious, and He wants us to experience the same kind of soul-filling joy so that we can bear fruit through it. But He reminds us that true joy is found in Him and can only be maintained when we keep Him at the center of our lives.

The Holy Spirit is also a source of joy, as He is our comforter and guide. He is with us every step of the way, reminding us that we are never alone and showing us how to go through difficult times with courage and strength. When we find ourselves in a place of fear or worry, the Spirit brings us back to the joy we find in God's presence.

Of the fruit listed in Galatians, joy is the one that can be the most elusive. Yet it's also the one we need the most, as it brings us back to a place of peace and hope. And when we seek God as the primary source of our joy, it overflows through our lives and into the lives of those around us.

We show love to those who need it, comfort those who are hurting, and spread the gospel's good news. Suddenly, there is no stranger or enemy, only brothers, and sisters who are worthy of feeling the deep joy that comes from knowing the love of God.

The Psalms give us a glimpse into how to cultivate joy in our lives. They remind us that true joy is found in praising the Lord and meditating on His word. Psalm 100:2 says, "Serve the Lord with gladness; come into His presence with singing!" This is a call to actively seek out joy by celebrating God's goodness, mercy, and grace.

Another says, "Delight yourself in the Lord, and He will give you the desires of your heart." When we set our minds on joy, God will give us the strength to pursue it relentlessly.

The fruit of the Spirit, joy, can seem like an elusive goal to strive towards. But it is one that we should all strive for, as it brings us into a place of peace and hope that can only be found in Christ.

We then find the strength to keep going even when things seem impossible. And when we allow joy to fill our hearts, we can go out into the world with courage and confidence, knowing that God is on our side!

SCRIPTURES TO MEDITATE ON

Galatians 5:22-23: "But the fruit of the Spirit is love, joy, peace, patience, kindness, goodness, faithfulness, gentleness, self-control; against such things, there is no law."

- ______________________________
- ______________________________

Philippians 4:4: "Rejoice in the Lord always. I will say it again: Rejoice!"

- ______________________________
- ______________________________

John 15:11: "These things I have spoken to you, that My joy may remain in you, and that your joy may be full."

- ______________________________
- ______________________________

5 STATEMENTS TO MEASURE THE FRUIT OF JOY

✳ I seek out moments of joy rather than dwelling on sadness or worry.
✳ I am quick to share a kind word or encouraging gesture with those around me.
✳ I look for God's presence and blessings in all areas of my life.
✳ I focus on the positive aspects of my circumstances, even when things are difficult.
✳ I seek out intentional, joyful moments to share with my family and friends.

REFLECTION QUESTIONS

1. How has joy been missing from my life lately? Why?

✳ _____

✳ _____

2. What steps can I take to draw closer to God, the source of ultimate joy?

✳ _____

✳ _____

3. How can I bring more joy into my home, workplace, and community?

✳ _____

✳ _____

4. Who do I know who is struggling with sadness or despair right now? How can I share God's joy with them?

✳ _____

✳ _____

How to Increase Joy in...

MYSELF

When it comes to the fruit of joy, we all have different things that help us experience it more fully. For some people, it might be spending time in nature, listening to music, or being around friends. Others might find joy in their work or in helping others. The important thing is that we take the time to discover what makes us happy and then do more of those things.

One way to increase joy in our lives is to be intentional about it. We can set aside time each day to focus on the things that make us happy, whether reading our favorite book, taking a walk in nature, or praying and meditating on God's Word. When we make a habit of seeking out joy, it starts to overflow into every area of our lives.

We can also find joy by giving thanks for the good things that happen, even when they seem small. When we take the time to count our blessings, it puts everything into perspective and reminds us of how much good is in the world. And finally, we can remember that Jesus is always with us, no matter what we're going through. He is the source of our strength and comfort; when we allow Him into our lives, joy will be right there with Him.

YOUR CHURCH

Your church is a great place to demonstrate the fruit of joy! We can do this in many different ways, such as by creating opportunities for fellowship and service. When we come together with people who have similar beliefs, it's natural to share stories and experiences that bring us joy. We can also look for ways to serve the community and share God's love with those around us.

We can also use our church to celebrate joyous occasions, like baptisms or graduations. We can create space for people to express their emotions in a safe, comfortable environment. And finally, we can find ways to spread joy even in difficult times. We can pray for those who are grieving and offer words of comfort and support.

Above all, we should be mindful that joy is more than just a feeling—it's a way of life, a way to show God's love.

THE WORLD

We can spread joy to the world by showing kindness to everyone we encounter, no matter where they're from or their beliefs. We can use our words to encourage rather than criticize, and we can use our resources to help those in need. We can also look for ways to bridge divides between people of different backgrounds and cultures, finding common ground rather than differences. This can look like joining a local civic organization, talking to people in our community, or advocating for justice and equality.

When we're intentional about spreading joy, it has a ripple effect that can reach far beyond our own lives. We can be hopeful, knowing that even if the world seems dark at times, there is always light to be found when we open our hearts to the joy that God offers us.

Above all, we can remember that joy is a gift from God meant to be shared freely with the world. As believers, it's up to us to show the world what true joy looks like and spread it to everyone we meet. In a world seeking to separate us, let's be united in joy.

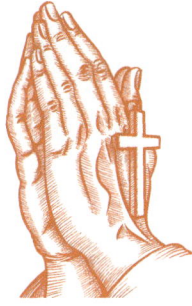

CLOSING PRAYER

Dear God, thank you for giving us the gift of joy. You are the source of true joy, and we are so thankful for Your presence in our lives. Help us to spread the joy You instill in us to those around us, no matter their background or beliefs. May we be mindful of how our words and actions affect others and use them to bring more joy into the world. And when we find ourselves in moments of sadness or despair, remind us to turn to You for comfort and reassurance. We pray all of this in Jesus' name, Amen.

WEEK 9:
PEACE:
A LASTING
FRUIT OF
THE SPIRIT

QUOTABLES

"Peace is the deep, inner, eternal stability the believer possesses by virtue of relationship with Jesus, a sense of balance that's not subject to external circumstance. It's also the quality that enables us to live harmoniously with others."

— Priscilla Shirer

WEEK 9 PEACE: A LASTING FRUIT OF THE SPIRIT

Flip open your phone or turn on the TV, and you'll see it: the world is a chaotic place. Stress, violence, and unrest can seem overwhelming. Global conflicts, climate change, and economic disparities—they all have an impact on our collective well-being.

Before we can start our days, anxieties and worries fill our minds. Too much of this can eventually drain us. As a result, we may feel helpless, and unable to do anything meaningful to make a difference in the world. Before long, a lack of peace will turn into bitterness, resentment, and anger.

But our faith tells us that it doesn't have to be this way! Jesus promised his disciples in John 14:27 that they would find peace—not just any kind of peace, but a lasting peace. The Bible also says that " the fruit of the Spirit is love, joy, peace, patience, kindness, goodness, faithfulness, gentleness and self-control" (Galatians 5:22). Fruit growing from a vine must be cultivated and nurtured, but the fruit of peace is lasting.

The fruit of the Spirit is a great starting point—it contains nine attributes, one of which is peace (Galatians 5:22-23). This peace isn't just any kind of peacefulness; it is a deep and abiding peace that goes beyond our comprehension. It stems from the presence of God in our lives, and it does not depend on the chaos of the world around us. It grows from our relationship with Jesus—the Prince of Peace (Isaiah 9:6).

122

Scripture has much to say about this fruit of the Spirit:

Isaiah 32:17 says, "The fruit of righteousness will be peace; the effect of righteousness will be quietness and confidence forever."

Philippians 4:7 also tells us, "And the peace of God, which surpasses all understanding, will guard your hearts and minds through Christ Jesus."

Jesus Himself said in John 14:27, "Peace I leave with you; my peace I give to you. Not as the world gives do I give to you. Let not your hearts be troubled, neither let them be afraid." He knew that those who follow Him would face turbulence and trouble, but He gives us His peace as a comforting assurance that He is with us in whatever we face.

We begin to search for this peace when we recognize that Jesus is the prince of peace—the only one who can provide true and lasting peace in our lives (Isaiah 9:6). And as the prince of peace, we can trust that He will give us the peace that surpasses all understanding, no matter what we are facing.

So how can we know that peace is truly starting to grow in us? The Bible tells us how peace works within us:

1. We are able to obey God in difficult circumstances (Romans 12:18).

2. We trust that God is ultimately in control, and His will will prevail (Proverbs 3:5-6).

3. We focus our thoughts away from worry and onto ways we can serve Him (Philippians 4:8).

4. We seek to be reconciled with others and make peace wherever possible (Matthew 5:9).

5. We are content in our current situation, trusting that God will provide for us (Hebrews 13:5-6).

Knowing this peace within ourselves can then lead us to the next step of cultivating it in our lives - becoming an ambassador for peace in our world. Consider the many issues that face our world, and think about how practicing the fruit of peace can bring a lasting solution to these issues. Imagine how peace can bring people together and bring about lasting change in our world.

Paul - who wrote the letter to the Corinthians - knew a thing or two about peace. He admonished the church there to "let a man of peace be in charge of you," (1 Corinthians 14:33), and he himself was known as one who promoted peace among all people. Even when his life was on the line, he chose peace and reconciliation. He knew that the source of true peace was in Christ, and this knowledge helped him become a peacemaker for his community. And knowing that, we can become beacons of peace in our own worlds.

We all need God's peace in our lives, and He is always ready to give it to us when we ask. Using Paul's example, let us strive to increase this fruit in our own lives and then impact those around us. Only then can we truly experience peace and bring it to the world.

SCRIPTURES TO MEDITATE ON

Isaiah 32:17 (NIV): "The fruit of righteousness will be peace; the effect of righteousness will be quietness and confidence forever."

✖ _____

✖ _____

Philippians 4:7 (NIV): "And the peace of God, which transcends all understanding, will guard your hearts and minds in Christ Jesus."

✖ _____

✖ _____

124

John 14:27 (NIV): "Peace I leave with you; my peace I give you. I do not give to you as the world gives. Do not let your hearts be troubled and do not be afraid."

- ______________________________
- ______________________________

Isaiah 9:6 (NIV): "For to us a child is born, to us a son is given, and the government will be on his shoulders. And he will be called Wonderful Counselor, Mighty God, Everlasting Father, Prince of Peace."

- ______________________________
- ______________________________

5 STATEMENTS TO MEASURE THE FRUIT OF PEACE

- I know that God is the giver of peace when I am able to find inner peace and contentment, despite the chaos around me.
- My heart is not troubled or afraid even in difficult situations, and I experience the supernatural peace of God.
- I trust in Christ, no matter what happens, and seek to be an ambassador of peace wherever I go.
- When faced with difficult situations or conflicts, I try to bring reconciliation and promote peace.
- I strive to keep the peace in my relationships and community by being a peacemaker and avoiding strife.

REFLECTION QUESTIONS

1. When have I experienced the peace of God in my life? What was happening?

※ ______________________________

※ ______________________________

2. How can I become an ambassador of peace in my community and relationships?

※ ______________________________

※ ______________________________

3. What is one practical step I can take today to increase the fruit of peace in my life?

※ ______________________________

※ ______________________________

4. Is there a situation or relationship where I need to bring peace this week?

※ ______________________________

※ ______________________________

How to Increase Peace in...

MYSELF

There are many ways we can cultivate biblical peace in our lives. One way is to spend time with God through prayer and reading his Word. When we spend time with him, we learn to trust him more and find his peace that surpasses all understanding. We can also find peace by spending time in nature or simply resting and focusing on our breath. Practicing these things on a regular basis will help us to experience biblical peace more consistently in our lives.

Another way to cultivate peace is by practicing forgiveness. Forgiveness doesn't mean that we forget what has happened, but it does mean that we choose to release the hurt and anger and move forward in love. Forgiving others allows us to experience the freedom that comes from releasing bitterness and resentment, and this, in turn, brings inner peace.

Finally, we can cultivate biblical peace by practicing kindness and compassion towards others. When we extend compassion to those who are hurting, it helps to ease our own hearts and allows us to experience the peace of God more fully. By choosing to be kind instead of judgmental, we create an atmosphere of love and peace that extends out into the world around us. Knowing how to extend peace to those around us also helps us cultivate inner peace.

YOUR CHURCH

One of the best ways to cultivate peace in our church is by creating an environment of love and acceptance. When we welcome everyone, regardless of their race, religion, or socio-economic status, we show that we value peace and diversity. We can also create a peaceful environment by practicing hospitality. Opening our doors and hearts to others allows them to feel loved and accepted, which can help ease any tensions that may be present.

Another way to cultivate peace in our church is by being forgiving. This doesn't mean that we have to agree with everything that someone has done, but it does mean that we choose to extend compassion and understanding. Doing this helps heal any wounds that may have been inflicted and allows us to move forward in love. Finally, we can promote peace in our church by simply being kind to one another. When we choose to be loving instead of judgmental, it helps to create an atmosphere of peace and healing.

THE WORLD

When it comes to cultivating peace in the world, one of the most important things we can do is extend love and compassion to those suffering. This means reaching out with kindness and understanding instead of judgment and condemnation. We can also promote peace

by speaking up for justice and equality, especially when people are being treated unfairly. When we stand up for what is right, it helps to create an atmosphere of fairness and respect that can lead to peace.

Our world is plagued by violence, hatred, and division. One of the best ways to combat this is by understanding our differences and celebrating them. We can do this by learning about different cultures and beliefs so that we can better understand each other's perspectives. When we choose to embrace diversity instead of fear it, we create an atmosphere of peace and understanding.

When we know inner peace, we can pour out that peace into the world around us. May we all strive to live lives of peace and love so that we can extend this blessing out into our hurting world!

CLOSING PRAYER

Heavenly Father, we thank you for the peace that comes from knowing you. We ask that you help us to cultivate this peace in our lives and extend it out into our churches and our world. Give us the courage to stand up for justice, practice forgiveness, and show kindness to those who are suffering. May your peace and love reign in our hearts and throughout the world. In Jesus' name we pray, Amen.

WEEK 10: PATIENCE: TRUSTING IN GOD'S DIVINE TIMING

QUOTABLES

Blessed is the grace of patience, but hard is it to be acquired. May the Lord, of His infinite mercy, teach us to bear all His holy will, and bear it cheerfully, and so to take up our cross for Jesus' sake!"

— Charles Spurgeon

WEEK 10 PATIENCE: TRUSTING IN GOD'S DIVINE TIMING

Would you say that you are a *patient* person?

Think of your daily life: How do you react to having to wait? Do you get frustrated during delays, or can you remain calm in the face of uncertainty? Are you calm with people who are different than you?

The Bible tells us to be patient in all things, and that patience is a fruit of the Spirit. Galatians 5:22-23 says, "But the fruit of the Spirit is love, joy, peace, forbearance, kindness, goodness, faithfulness, gentleness, and self-control."

Patience is important because it is trusting in God's divine timing and His perfect plan, even when we don't understand it or can't see the end result. When we are patient with others, especially those different than us, it helps create an environment of understanding and grace that encourages diversity, equity, and inclusion with our fellow humans.

This is exactly what God wants from all of us. He asks that we trust his divine timing and be patient as he works out whatever situation you may come across.

The Bible repeatedly speaks to our need for patience, reminding us to keep a steady heart and trust in God's good timing. Hebrews 10:36 says, "For you have need of endurance, so that when you have done the will of God you may receive what is promised." Similarly, Proverbs 16:32 states,

"Better to be patient than powerful; better to have self-control than to conquer a city."

But patience can be hard to find in our have-it-now culture. To cultivate patience, it's important to remember that our lives are God's stories to tell, not ours. As we go through life, we can trust that the Lord will bring us peace and contentment as he leads us in the right direction.

Jesus taught on patience in many ways and talked about the need for faith to live out patience. He said in Matthew 24:13, "But he who endures to the end will be saved." Jesus was also a patient teacher and leader, often taking time to explain things slowly and patiently, allowing his followers time to understand and comprehend his teachings. Even when his apostles would have been quick to anger or defend themselves, Jesus was always patient and understanding.

What are some practical ways that we can increase this fruit of the Spirit in our lives? To grow in patience, it's important to remember that God is always sovereign and in control. He is never surprised by any situation, and he has a plan for us, even if we cannot see it.

This is why patience is included with the other fruits of the spirit, such as love and joy. Only when we see patience as a way to live out our faith can we begin to understand it more deeply. To have patience, we must trust in God's divine timing and rest in the assurance that his plans are perfect.

And consider how patient God is with us! He is "not willing that any should perish, but that all should come to repentance" (2 Peter 3:9). He desires for us to turn to Him and seek him out, not just in times of difficulty but also when we are living in joy. When we continually seek Him and ask for His guidance, we can rest assured that He will never abandon us.

As Christians, it's our duty to be patient with ourselves and others, even when we may feel tired or

©2023 La'Wana Harris, Inc All Rights Reserved.

anxious. Only when we trust in the Lord's divine timing can we truly understand patience as He intended it - as a reflection of our faith.

When we feel like we're running out of patience, it's essential to stop and remember that God is in control. We can let go of our worries, knowing that His plans are perfect and that He will make all things right in His own time. We can increase this fruit of the Spirit in our lives by spending more time praying, meditating on Scripture, and developing a closer relationship with God. We can also practice patience and understanding in our relationships with others and find ways to be patient when facing challenging situations.

SCRIPTURES TO MEDITATE ON

Isaiah 40:31 "But they who wait for the Lord shall renew their strength; they shall mount up with wings like eagles; they shall run and not be weary; they shall walk and not faint."

❖ _____

❖ _____

Lamentations 3:26 "It is good that one should wait quietly for the salvation of the Lord."

❖ _____

❖ _____

Romans 12:12 "Rejoice in hope, be patient in tribulation, be constant in prayer."

❖ _____

❖ _____

Matthew 24:13 "But he who endures to the end will be saved."

�֍ _____

✖ _____

5 STATEMENTS TO MEASURE THE FRUIT OF PEACE

✖ I will find times in my busy day to practice patience and trust in God's timing.

✖ I will be patient with others, regardless of their opinions or beliefs.

✖ I will choose kindness over criticism when I am feeling impatient.

✖ I will remember that God is always in control, even in difficult times.

✖ I will seek out practical ways to increase my understanding of patience.

REFLECTION QUESTIONS

1. How does my lack of patience affect my relationships with others?

✖ _____

✖ _____

2. How can I practice patience in challenging situations?

✖ _____

✖ _____

3. What Scripture passages can remind me to be patient with myself and others?

✖ _____

✖ _____

4. In what ways has God been faithful and patient with me in the past?

- ______________________________
- ______________________________

How to Increase Patience in...

MYSELF

Patience is a fruit of the Spirit that can be cultivated through prayer, meditation, and spending time with God. When we focus on our relationship with Him, we are able to grow in other areas of our lives as well.

We can also increase our patience by setting realistic expectations for ourselves and others. We are less likely to become frustrated or angry when we understand that everyone makes mistakes. We can also practice self-compassion, forgiving ourselves when we mess up.

It's also important to take some time for ourselves every day. This can be done through activities such as reading, walking, or listening to music. This allows us to relax and recharge so that we are able to approach challenging situations with a more positive attitude.

When it comes to dealing with others, patience is key. It's important to be understanding and accepting of others, even when they don't think or act the way we do. We should also remember that everyone has their own journey in life, and it's not our place to judge them.

When we are patient with others, it shows them that we care about them and want them to succeed. It also creates a more calm and peaceful environment, which is beneficial for all involved.

YOUR CHURCH

Patience is an incredibly important virtue in the church. Not only is it a reflection of our relationship with God, but it also sets an example for others.

One way churches can encourage patience is by emphasizing the importance of community and understanding among different groups within the congregation. This could include bridging generational gaps or creating more inclusive spaces for diverse beliefs and practices.

The church should also strive to create a welcoming and patient environment for newcomers. This could be done by training ushers, greeters, and hospitality teams on the importance of providing an open and accepting atmosphere. Additionally, churches can provide resources such as support groups or mentorship programs that focus on building relationships with others through patience and understanding.

When the church can demonstrate patience and love to its members, it can help foster a sense of belonging. This can make all the difference in someone's life, as they may be looking for an accepting place to turn to during difficult times.

THE WORLD

The world is becoming increasingly diverse, and with this comes both opportunities and challenges. In order for us to create a more tolerant and accepting global community, we must learn how to practice patience with those who are different from us.

The best way to do this is by educating ourselves on other cultures and beliefs. We can also get involved in organizations that focus on promoting understanding and acceptance between people of different backgrounds. Additionally, we can seek out opportunities to interact with people of different cultures and beliefs, such as attending multicultural events or volunteering in our communities.

By taking the time to learn more about others and their perspectives, we can develop a greater understanding of how patience plays a vital role in creating a peaceful world. We must strive to recognize that everyone has something valuable to bring to the table and that we are all connected in some way.

By cultivating patience, we can create a better world for everyone. We can show love and acceptance to those around us, regardless of their differences.

As the Bible says, "Be patient, therefore, brothers, until the coming of the Lord. See how the farmer waits for the precious fruit of the earth, being patient about it, until it receives the early and the late rains" (James 5:7).

Let us all strive to practice patience in our own lives and within our communities. May we learn from each other so that we can build a more peaceful world together.

CLOSING PRAYER

Father God, we thank you for your patience and grace. Help us to be patient with ourselves and those around us so that we may create a more understanding world in your name. May we seek to accept and love all people, regardless of their differences. And when times get tough, help us to remember that patience brings understanding and peace. In Jesus' Name, Amen.

WEEK 11: KINDNESS: POURING OUT GOD'S GRACE

QUOTABLES

O child of God, be more careful to keep the way of the Lord, more concentrated in heart in seeking His glory, and you will see the loving-kindness and the tender mercy of the Lord in your life.

— Charles Spurgeon

WEEK 11 KINDNESS: POURING OUT GOD'S GRACE

Kindness is a virtue that seems to have gone missing in the past few years. Flip on the television, jump on social media, and you see a world filled with cynicism and criticism. We're all so quick to judge, criticize, and tear each other down. It can feel as though we have forgotten how to show basic human kindness.

But the Bible tells us that showing kindness is a fruit of the Spirit, and if we're to reflect the character of God, then we must practice this virtue. We see kindness throughout the Bible, from God's actions towards us to the way Jesus treated others. Romans 2:4 says, "Or do you show contempt for the riches of his kindness, forbearance, and patience?"

The Bible speaks of kindness across the pages. In Ephesians 4:32, "Be kind and compassionate to one another, forgiving each other, just as in Christ God forgave you." Proverbs 3:3 says, "Let love and faithfulness never leave you; bind them around your neck, write them on the tablet of your heart."

And 1 Peter 3:8 says, "Finally, all of you should be of one mind. Sympathize with each other. Love each other as brothers and sisters. Be tenderhearted, and keep a humble attitude."

It's clear that God has called us to a life of kindness. But why? We need to understand that when we show kindness, we're pouring out God's grace into our lives and the lives of those around us. Kindness is a reflection of our faith; it's an outward expression of what lies within our hearts- love for others just as Jesus has love for us.

Think of some of the significant characters in the Bible. Abraham is remembered for his hospitality, Esther for her courage and willingness to sacrifice for others, Joseph for his faith and trust in God, and Paul for his boldness in sharing the Good News. These are all expressions of kindness that come from a deep place in our faith journey.

Most importantly, we have the perfect example of kindness in Jesus. He showed kindness to the outcasts, the poor, and even to his enemies. We must measure our own obedience and faithfulness against the example that he has set.

One example of this comes from a passage in John 8:1-11. Jesus was surrounded by crowds who were ready to stone an adulterous woman, and yet he showed mercy, compassion, and kindness in his response. When others saw her as an outcast, Jesus saw her as a beloved child of God. Instead of punishing her, he offered her forgiveness.

Kindness can be hard to find when our hearts aren't in tune with God. But if we will seek and practice kindness, then we must look for ways to show compassion, mercy, grace, and love to those around us. Only when we understand this fruit as the reflection of God's grace can we truly live out our faith.

SCRIPTURES TO MEDITATE ON

Matthew 5:7, "Blessed are the merciful, for they will be shown mercy."

❋ _____

❋ _____

Proverbs 11:17, "The kind man does himself good, but the cruel man hurts himself."

❋ _____

❋ _____

Luke 6:36, "Be kind and compassionate to one another, forgiving each other, just as in Christ God forgave you."

❋ _____

❋ _____

Ephesians 4:32, "Be kind and compassionate to one another, forgiving each other, just as in Christ God forgave you."

❋ _____

❋ _____

1 Peter 3:8-9, "Finally, all of you should be of one mind. Sympathize with each other. Love each other as brothers and sisters. Be tenderhearted, and keep a humble attitude. Do not repay evil with evil or insult with insult. On the contrary, repay evil with blessing, because to this you were called so that you may inherit a blessing."

❋ _____

❋ _____

5 STATEMENTS TO MEASURE THE FRUIT OF KINDNESS

- I will seek to grow in patience in small, everyday ways.
- I will seek to show kindness, compassion, and mercy in all my relationships.
- I will practice empathy by listening with understanding and not just hearing.
- I will strive to put others' needs before my own in every situation.
- I will work towards showing respect for everyone regardless of age, race, gender, or culture.

REFLECTION QUESTIONS

What areas of my life do I need to be more mindful of showing kindness?

- ______________________________
- ______________________________

In what ways can I practice kindness daily in all my relationships?

- ______________________________
- ______________________________

How can I extend grace and love to those who may not deserve it?

- ______________________________
- ______________________________

How can I invite God's mercy into difficult situations?

- ______________________________
- ______________________________

How to Increase Kindness in...

MYSELF

When it comes to cultivating kindness in our lives, there are a few things we can do to help get us started. First, we need to be patient with ourselves. We're all on a journey, and we won't be perfect at showing kindness all the time. But if we start small and work towards being more patient in everyday situations, then we're on the right track.

Second, we should be kind to those around us. This doesn't mean that we have to go out of our way to please everyone, but by simply being kind and compassionate, we can make a big difference in someone's day.

Third, we should forgive others. This is a difficult task, but it's so vital if we want to cultivate a heart of kindness. When we forgive others, it shows that we understand that everyone makes mistakes and that we're willing to move forward in a positive way.

Fourth, try to put yourself in other people's shoes. Empathy is such an important part of kindness, and by trying to see things from another person's perspective, we can better understand their situation.

Finally, show respect for everyone, regardless of who they are or their beliefs. Everyone deserves to be treated with dignity and respect, and by doing this, we can help break down the barriers that divide us.

YOUR CHURCH

The church should be one of the main locations where kindness flows. Unfortunately, the church can often be a place of judgment and harshness. Many enter the doors of a church looking for a place of acceptance and understanding, but instead, they find criticism and exclusion.

To increase kindness in the church, we must first make sure that everyone is welcomed and accepted regardless of race, gender, or background. We should strive to create an atmosphere where no one feels left out or judged for their beliefs.

Second, we must make sure that kindness is part of the church's mission statement. Kindness should not be something that happens by chance but rather a priority in the church's culture.

Third, we can create programs and activities within the church to emphasize the importance of kindness. These could include service projects, Bible studies on compassion and understanding, or even a weekly gathering of members to discuss how kindness has affected their lives.

Finally, we should all strive to model kindness in our own lives. As the saying goes, "Actions speak louder than words." If we want others to be kind, then we must first show them what it looks like.

THE WORLD

Would you agree that our world needs more kindness? It's no secret that we live in a world full of hatred and division. But there are things we can do to help bring kindness back into the world - and when we do, it can have a ripple effect.

First and foremost, we must strive to be kind to ourselves. Like many things in life, kindness begins within each of us. We must learn to practice patience and understanding, especially when it comes to those who may not share our beliefs.

Second, we should look for the good in others. This can be difficult as we are often taught to focus on differences rather than similarities. But if we train ourselves to look for the good in others, it can tremendously impact how we see and interact with them.

We should stand up against bullies. Unfortunately, bullying has become an epidemic, destroying the lives of many of all ages. If we witness bullying and stand up against it, then we can help create an atmosphere of kindness and compassion.

Finally, we need to encourage more dialogue between opposing sides. We can all agree that it's easy to hate someone without ever really knowing them. If we take the time to listen and understand one another, we may find common ground and eventually break down the walls of hostility.

147

CLOSING PRAYER

Lord God, thank you for teaching us the importance of kindness. Help us to be compassionate and understanding towards those around us, even when it's difficult. Guide our hearts so that we may spread kindness not only in our own lives but throughout the world. And may we all strive to live lives that are truly worthy of your love. In Jesus' name, Amen.

WEEK 12: GOODNESS: A GOOD FATHER WHO LOVES US

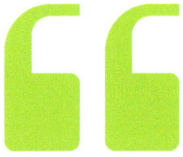

QUOTABLES

All the goodness I have within me is totally from the Lord alone. When I sin, it is from me and is done on my own, but when I act righteously, it is wholly and completely of God.

-Charles Spurgeon

WEEK 12 GOODNESS: A GOOD FATHER WHO LOVES US

⊙

"*Oh, goodness!*" We've all sighed and said this phrase in a moment of relief or surprise. But what do we mean when we say "goodness"? Do we truly understand what it means to be good?

The Fruit of the Spirit can help us answer this question. Galatians 5:22-23 lists nine fruits of the spirit: love, joy, peace, patience, kindness, goodness, faithfulness, gentleness, and self-control. Of these nine fruits, we will focus on Goodness today.

Goodness is defined as "the quality of being good." So what does it mean to be good? A question that mankind has searched for the answer to. The Bible helps us understand it better. Psalm 31:19 says, "Oh, how abundant is your goodness, which you have stored up for those who fear You and worked for those who take refuge in You." God's goodness is a part of His love towards us and shows that He is a good Father who loves us.

Consider those in the Bible who have demonstrated the Fruit of Goodness. Moses, Noah, and Abraham were all examples of those who showed goodness to those around them despite their circumstances.

Noah found favor in God's eyes, despite the wickedness of his generation. He was obedient to God and followed His commands. In his obedience to build the ark, he showed goodness to God, his family, and all of creation.

Moses was a leader who showed courage and mercy to the

151

Israelites in the face of tremendous difficulties. His faithfulness toward God is unparalleled, and his obedience demonstrates what it means to be good.

Abraham demonstrated his deep love for God by being willing to sacrifice his son Isaac. His unwavering faith in God's goodness demonstrates the power of being good.

Jesus, Himself shows us how goodness and love can be intertwined. He showed immense mercy to those around Him and always chose the path of righteousness. One example of His goodness is found in his conversation with the Samaritan woman. His love and acceptance of her despite her lifestyle choices - and her shock that He spoke to her - is a powerful reminder of what it means to be good.

As we strive for equity and inclusion in our churches, communities, and the world around us, it's important to remember that being good is an integral part of this process. When we seek the good in others, we are able to truly acknowledge their humanity and respect them as equals.

In a world that seems lost and unable to find its way, we can find peace and assurance in the knowledge that God is good. He loves us unconditionally and desires for us to live in unity with one another. This, in turn, will lead to greater understanding, compassion, and love.

How will you seek to find the good in others today? What practical ways can you demonstrate goodness to those around you? How can you share this knowledge with others when you begin to recognize what it means to be good?

May we seek ways to increase the goodness in ourselves, our churches, and the world around us. May we embrace God's love and share it with others. Our world needs us to be the light of goodness in the darkness. May God bless you as you continue your journey of uncovering what it means to be good!

SCRIPTURES TO MEDITATE ON

Psalm 31:19: "Oh, how abundant is your goodness, which you have stored up for those who fear You and worked for those who take refuge in You."

- ______________________________
- ______________________________

Matthew 5:7: "Blessed are the merciful, for they will be shown mercy."

- ______________________________
- ______________________________

Genesis 18:19: "For I have chosen him, so that he may command his children and his household after him to keep the way of the Lord by doing righteousness and justice, so that the Lord may bring upon Abraham what He has spoken about him."

- ______________________________
- ______________________________

Luke 6:35-36: "But love your enemies, do good, and lend, expecting nothing in return; and your reward will be great, and you will be sons of the Most High. For He is kind to the unthankful and evil."

- ______________________________
- ______________________________

Proverbs 3:27: "Do not withhold good from those to whom it is due, when it is in your power to do it."

- ______________________________
- ______________________________

5 STATEMENTS TO MEASURE THE FRUIT OF GOODNESS

✖ I will look for ways to show goodness in my relationships with others.
✖ I will be intentional about extending grace and mercy to those who
✖ need it the most.
✖ I will strive to love my enemies, do good and lend, expecting nothing in return.
✖ I will look for ways to promote justice and righteousness in all areas of life.
✖ I will be generous with kindness and compassion towards others.

REFLECTION QUESTIONS

How can I show goodness in my relationships today?

✖ _____

✖ _____

What does it mean to be a good person in light of scripture?

✖ _____

✖ _____

In what ways can I extend mercy and grace to those around me?

✖ _____

✖ _____

How can I promote justice and righteousness in the world today?

✖ _____

✖ _____

How to Increase Goodness in...

MYSELF

Showing goodness to others begins with showing goodness to myself. This means engaging in self-care and setting healthy boundaries. It also involves being gentle with yourself, forgiving yourself when you make mistakes, and embracing the goodness God has given you.

One of the best ways to cultivate biblical goodness in our personal lives is by seeking opportunities to show others kindness and compassion. When we extend love and compassion to those who need it the most, we are living out the biblical mandate to love our neighbor as ourselves. We can also pray for God's love to fill us up so that we can pour out His love onto those around us.

Another way to grow in biblical goodness is by reading scriptures that focus on love and mercy. As we immerse ourselves in these passages, we will be drawn closer to God and His heart for compassion and goodness.

Finally, we can also look for ways to serve others in our community. This could involve volunteering at a local homeless shelter or food bank or working with refugees or immigrants. When we serve others selflessly, we are tangibly showing the love of Christ.

May we all seek ways to grow in biblical goodness and extend God's love to those around us. When we build a culture of service and love, God will be glorified, and His Kingdom will be advanced.

YOUR CHURCH

God has created the church to be an ambassador of His love and goodness. We are called to be the light of the world, a beacon of hope that points people to Jesus. To accomplish this, it is essential that we create a culture of belonging and acceptance within our churches.

We can strive for biblical goodness by intentionally seeking ways to build relationships with those different from us. This could include inviting members of different cultures, backgrounds, and ages to join us in worship or inviting diverse speakers to preach at our services. We can also create programs focusing on service and mercy towards those often marginalized in society.

Goodness can also take many forms. We can look for ways to serve our church members and the community. This could include providing meals, setting up transportation services, or offering other practical assistance. It is also important that we seek out opportunities to listen to marginalized people and make sure their voices are heard.

Finally, we should ensure that everyone has a seat at the table. This means striving for diversity and inclusion in all areas of church life. When we continue to seek out ways to extend love, kindness, and mercy toward others, our churches will be a place where goodness reigns supreme.

THE WORLD

The world can often be harsh, but God has called us to bring His light and hope into the darkness.

We are called to be reflections of His goodness, empowered by the Holy Spirit to show love and kindness in a broken world.

One way we can show God's goodness is by taking action on behalf of those who have been denied justice. We can use our time, talents, and resources to fight for the oppressed, advocate for the vulnerable, and support organizations that are working to promote justice.

We can also look for ways to start conversations about complex topics like racism, inequity, and injustice. We must choose our words carefully and ensure we are listening with an open heart and mind. When we create a safe space to have these discussions, we can move towards solutions that bring about positive change.

Finally, we must strive to be examples of God's love and goodness to those around us. We can extend grace and mercy, choose kindness over criticism, and show compassion even in the face of disagreement. When we live out the fruit of the Spirit in our everyday lives, the world will know that Jesus is alive and well.

CLOSING PRAYER

Heavenly Father, thank You for Your goodness and love. Help us to see how we can be reflections of Your character in our lives, our church, and our world. Empower us with Your Spirit to show kindness and mercy even when it is difficult. May the world experience Your love and grace through our words and actions. In Jesus' Name, Amen.

WEEK 13: FAITHFULNESS: STAYING TRUE NO MATTER WHAT

QUOTABLES

Often times God demonstrates His faithfulness in adversity by providing for us what we need to survive. He does not change our painful circumstances. He sustains us through them.

— Charles Stanley

WEEK 13 FAITHFULNESS: STAYING TRUE NO MATTER WHAT

When we think of faithfulness, we often think of loyalty and trustworthiness. We may think of a friend who has stuck with us through thick and thin or a partner who has remained committed to us for years. Perhaps we even think of a faithful dog, always there and willing to lend unconditional love.

No matter what the idea of "faithfulness" evokes, it's a characteristic that brings us peace, joy, and even security. It's also a fruit of the Spirit, a part of the lifestyle of those who follow Christ.

The Bible speaks of faithfulness in many places, including Proverbs 3:3-4 (NKJV) which says, "Let not mercy and truth forsake you; bind them around your neck, write them on the tablet of your heart, and so find favor and high esteem in the sight of God and man."

In the New Testament, 1 Corinthians 4:2 (NIV) says, "Now it is required that those who have been given a trust must prove faithful." So whether we are entrusted with something physical or spiritual, faithfulness is essential in order to show ourselves as worthy of trust.

We often take for granted just how faithful God has been to us in our lives. Think of the many times you have forgotten God's promises, and yet He still stands with you. His faithfulness never fails. He is always ready to provide us with grace, mercy, and love.

It can be difficult to remain faithful in a world that values short-term success, instant gratification, and unrealistic expectations. But faithfulness is steadfast; it sticks with you no matter what comes your way.

Cultivating faithfulness requires we know what it looks like in our lives and how to stay committed in good and bad times. Not sure how to measure where you line up with God's definition of faithfulness? See how you react to these statements:

- I remain true to my word and do what I say.
- I am loyal in all relationships, no matter the cost.
- I look for ways to serve even when it's hard, unpleasant, or inconvenient.
- I don't give up when things get tough.
- remain hopeful in spite of the odds.

Take some time to reflect on how you relate to each of these statements. Are there areas where you could be more faithful? What does it look like for you to stay true and loyal in all situations?

In the Bible, we read of several examples of faithfulness:

Noah: Having been saved through the flood, Noah built an altar and made sacrifices to the Lord (Genesis 8:20-22).

Abraham: God told Abraham that his descendants would be as numerous as the stars in the sky. Though he was 100 years old and childless, Abraham still trusted God's promise of a great nation (Genesis 15:5-6).

Ruth: Ruth was a widow who had no reason to remain loyal to her mother-in-law. Instead, she chose faithfulness and stayed with Naomi despite the hard times they faced (Ruth 1:16).

Paul: Paul experienced many hardships in his journey of faith, but he remained faithful to the calling of God and was an example of steadfastness throughout his life (2 Corinthians 4:8-9).

We can learn much from these examples. And Jesus our Lord showcases what faithfulness looks like: no matter the cost, He was devoted to doing His Father's will. Jesus knew who He was in light of the Father's love and showed us that faithfulness is key to living a life of righteousness.

As we set out to increase our faithfulness, let us find ways to do this in ourselves, our church and our world. When we begin to reflect on the faithful nature of God, it brings glory to His name and the joy of His presence.

And here is the amazing part: faithfulness isn't something you have to try and muster up on your own. You can tap into the power of the Holy Spirit who works in you both to will and to do for His good pleasure (Philippians 2:13).

Take some time now to pray for God's grace to increase your faithfulness. May He fill us with the power and strength to remain steadfast in our relationships, commitments, and service to Him.

SCRIPTURES TO MEDITATE ON

Proverbs 3:3-4: Let not mercy and truth forsake you; bind them around your neck, write them on the tablet of your heart.

- ________________________
- ________________________

1 Corinthians 4:2: Now it is required that those who have been given a trust must prove faithful.

- ________________________
- ________________________

Hebrews 10:23: Let us hold unswervingly to the hope we profess, for he who promised is faithful.

❋ _____

❋ _____

2 Timothy 2:13: If we are faithless, he remains faithful--for he cannot disown himself.

❋ _____

❋ _____

5 STATEMENTS TO MEASURE THE FRUIT OF FAITHFULNESS

❋ I am faithful to the commitments and promises I make to God and others.

❋ I am willing to stick with things no matter how challenging they become.

❋ I recognize that being faithful is a form of obedience to God's commands.

❋ I know that faithfulness requires self-discipline, patience, and perseverance.

❋ I am willing to be humble and admit when I have not been faithful.

REFLECTION QUESTIONS

1. What areas of my life might require increased faithfulness?

❈ _____

❈ _____

2. How can I increase my faithfulness in those areas?

❈ _____

❈ _____

3. How have I been faithful to God and others this past week?

❈ _____

❈ _____

4. What can I do, moving forward, to live a life of faithfulness?

❈ _____

❈ _____

How to Increase Faithfulness in...

MYSELF

One key way to increase our faithfulness is to spend time with God in prayer and Scripture reading. As we come to know Him more deeply, we will be more likely to follow His commands and walk in His ways. We can also seek to cultivate disciplines that will help us stay faithful, such as being organized, setting healthy boundaries, and managing our time well.

Another essential way to increase faithfulness is by building relationships with others who are also committed to walking faithfully with God. Surrounding ourselves with like-minded individuals encourages us to stay strong in our faith and grow in maturity.

Finally, we can ask the Holy Spirit to help us be more faithful in all that we do. He desires for us to be steadfast and obedient, and He will give us the strength we need to accomplish great things for His kingdom. Let us pray for Him to increase our faithfulness so that we may honor Him with our lives. When we live in complete devotion to God and put our trust in Him, He will be faithful to us even when we are not.

YOUR CHURCH

Many in our world are seeking true faithfulness, and our churches can be the place where they find it. Churches should strive to be places of refuge for those struggling with faithlessness in their lives, offering them acceptance and love. We must also remember that faithful people build strong communities and create a culture of hospitality that welcomes everyone.

To increase faithfulness in our churches, we must first commit to praying for our churches, our leaders, and one another. We then need to model faithfulness in our lives by being faithful in prayer, giving, attending church services regularly, and participating in community activities that encourage fellowship and growth in the Lord. We can also show faithfulness by engaging in meaningful conversations with those around us, listening to their stories, and being willing to serve one another humbly.

When we lack the faithfulness to stay committed to our church communities, it can be a sign that something needs to change. We must prayerfully seek God's guidance and discern what that change might be. He will lead us in the right way as we strive to serve Him faithfully in our churches.

THE WORLD

For faithfulness to spread from our hearts to our world, we must start by living faithfully. This means walking in obedience to God's commands, being diligent about doing good works that honor Him, and following His guidance even when it is difficult. We must also be willing to participate in ministries and organizations that reach out to the hurting, the poor, and those in need of hope.

Giving others who don't know God an example of faithfulness can be a powerful witness to them. They may come to see that there is something different about us and be curious to learn more about our faith. We must also remember that being faithful means speaking up for those who are oppressed and marginalized, standing up for justice and equality in our world, and advocating for the fundamental human rights of all people.

CLOSING PRAYER

Lord, we ask that You would increase our faithfulness and help us remain steadfast in all that we do. We desire to honor You with our lives and know that You will be faithful to us even when we are not. Guide our steps as we seek to live faithfully so that others may see Your glory in us and come to know You more deeply. Please lead us to ministries and organizations that will help spread Your faithfulness throughout our world. In Jesus' name, Amen.

WEEK 14: GENTLENESS: CHOOSING PEACE OVER CONFLICT

QUOTABLES

Perhaps no grace is less prayed for, or less cultivated than gentleness. Indeed it is considered rather as belonging to natural disposition or external manners, than as a Christian virtue; and seldom do we reflect that not to be gentle is sin.

— George Bethune

WEEK 14 GENTLENESS: CHOOSING PEACE OVER CONFLICT

In our world, we often think that "might makes right" - that those who are loudest and strongest will win. But the Bible tells a different story. In the kingdom of God, those who seek to lead with gentleness have true power.

Does it sound crazy? It might seem as though gentleness is a sign of weakness, but it's not. Gentleness is actually a Fruit of the Spirit that the Apostle Paul taught us to live out (Galatians 5:22-23). Within this list of fruits, gentleness is actually a sign of strength.

To understand how gentleness is both strong and powerful, we need to look at what gentleness is not:

- Gentleness is not passively allowing harm or injustice to happen.
- Gentleness is not failing to stand up for what is right.
- Gentleness is not seeking to avoid conflict.

Rather, gentleness is choosing peace over conflict whenever possible. It has a humble spirit even in the face of challenging situations. And it's being willing to listen and learn before responding with actions or words.

In the Bible, we read of someone who embodied gentleness: Jesus. He was strong and powerful, yet gentle. He could have called legions of angels to fight for Him went the Pharisees and soldiers came to arrest Him in the garden of Gethsemane, but He chose to remain gentle.

In fact, it was Jesus' response in gentleness that took power away from the Pharisees. His gentleness was so powerful they couldn't even bring themselves to come near Him!

What do you think drove Jesus' gentle nature? Being God certainly helps, but He was also fully human. And if you've lived on earth for any length of time, you know that the potential for conflict is always present. But choosing gentleness doesn't mean we have to be doormats. Rather, it begins with knowing who we are to God.

As children of the Father, we can trust that He will take up our cause and fight for us. We can trust that even in the most difficult of circumstances, He will make a way. So when we stay focused on Him and His power, gentleness is an easier choice to make.

Imagine that! When we face even the most difficult and challenging of situations, gentleness is possible.

That's because God does not ask us to be strong in our own strength but His. This confidence can then flow out from us and make even the most difficult conversations easier to manage. It is only when we see that Biblical gentleness comes from our relationship with the Father that it is possible.

Where do you struggle to show gentleness in your daily life? Perhaps you are someone who is quick to anger or who likes to stand your ground in every disagreement. If that's the case, then it's time to look at yourself and see where you are seeking strength from.

Or maybe you find yourself unable to speak up for what is right. Gentleness does not have to compromise your convictions, but it does require you to come with a humble spirit. If you find yourself in this position, then take some time to pray and ask God for guidance on how to approach conversations and relationships from a place of gentleness.

No matter where we struggle, the

Fruit of the Spirit of Gentleness is achievable with God's help. We can choose gentleness over conflict and peace over strife - and it's there that we unlock the true power of God. And when we combine this fruit with the power of the others - love, joy, peace, patience, kindness, and self-control - the possibilities are truly endless.

Look for ways that you can apply gentleness to your life. Ask a trusted friend to reveal how you can be gentler in your relationships with others and yourself. And know that God is always there to give you the strength and grace necessary to live out His Fruit of Gentleness.

SCRIPTURES TO MEDITATE ON

Psalm 4:4: "Be angry, but do not sin; on your bed, search your heart and be still."

❋ _____

❋ _____

Ephesians 4:2: "With all humility and gentleness, with patience, bearing with one another in love."

❋ _____

❋ _____

Matthew 11:29: "Take my yoke upon you and learn from me, for I am gentle and humble in heart."

❋ _____

❋ _____

5 STATEMENTS TO MEASURE THE FRUIT OF GENTLENESS

- I strive to treat others with respect, even when I don't agree with them.
- I am willing to listen and consider other perspectives before responding.
- I choose peace over winning an argument.
  I remain humble, even when challenged or feeling attacked.
- I consider the feelings and needs of others before my own in a conflict
- situation.

REFLECTION QUESTIONS

1. What do I think of when I hear the word "gentleness"?

- ____________________
- ____________________

2. How do I react in difficult situations?

- ____________________
- ____________________

3. Do I tend to respond with gentleness or aggression?

- ____________________
- ____________________

4. What can I do to increase my gentleness in my everyday life with the help of the Holy Spirit?

- ____________________
- ____________________

How to Increase Gentleness in...

MYSELF

When it comes to cultivating gentleness in our lives, it's important that we start with ourselves. We need to be intentional about examining our own hearts and asking God to help us change any areas of unforgiveness, anger, or bitterness.

We also need to take the time to cultivate a spirit of humility. This means being teachable, admitting when we're wrong, and not always needing to be right. It also requires that we put the needs of others before our own.

In addition, we can pray for God's help in developing patience and kindness. These are essential components of gentleness. Consider the following as ways to increase gentleness in your own life:

- Spend time daily with God, listening to His voice and being open to His will.
- Practice self-care - take breaks from people or situations if need be so that you can remain focused on the Spirit of God rather than becoming overwhelmed by stress.
- Pray before responding to difficult situations.
- Ask for guidance from God and wise counsel from trusted friends before taking action.
- Seek forgiveness when needed, even if it's just in your heart.

YOUR CHURCH

The church is a spiritual home for many of us, and gentleness should be at the center of our interactions with one another there. We can encourage gentleness in our churches by modeling it ourselves and offering grace and patience to others.

We should also strive for unity in the church, which means that we extend understanding and mercy to those who disagree with us.

This includes listening and learning from each other's perspectives without judgment.

In addition, gentleness should be reflected in our church leadership. Leaders should be humble and approachable, not arrogant or dictatorial. We can pray for our pastors and leaders to lead with gentleness, understanding that God calls us to be kind to one another as we worship Him.

Our churches should become places where gentleness is not only accepted, but celebrated. We should strive for an atmosphere of grace and acceptance that reflects the heart of Jesus.

1. THE WORLD

In today's world, gentleness can seem like a lost art. But it doesn't have to be this way! We can choose to live with a spirit of gentleness and humility, even when faced with challenging situations. We can choose to be peacemakers in our own communities and around the world.

When we do this, we are demonstrating the love of Christ to others. We can be an example to those around us by showing them what it looks like to respond in a gentle manner. For instance, here are a few ways that we can live out gentleness in the world:

- Speak kindly to others and practice active listening.
- Treat those who disagree with us with respect.
- Lift up and encourage those around us instead of putting them down.
- Put the needs of others before our own.
- Lead by example, showing others how to live with gentleness and humility.

Can you imagine what our world would look like if we chose to live out this fruit of the Spirit instead of responding to difficult situations with aggression and anger? Tum sessed cuteremniur quam, ored nos Ahabem sertela publibus verfiri,

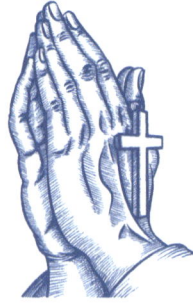

CLOSING PRAYER

Heavenly Father, thank You for Your gentleness towards us. Help us cultivate a spirit of humility and kindness within ourselves, our churches, and the world. Give us Your grace and strength to respond with gentleness in all things. May we be a reflection of Your love and compassion for those around us. In Jesus' Name, Amen.

WEEK 15:
SELF-CONTROL

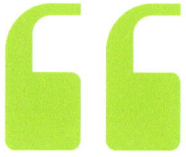

QUOTABLES

"To accomplish anything extraordinary you must blend desire for the goal with the will to take action to achieve it. This is how you commit to making yourself do what's right, whether you feel like it or not. The key is self-control."

— David Jeremiah

WEEK 15
SELF-CONTROL

The fruit of the spirit of self-control may be one of the most commonly misused and misunderstood gifts that God has given us. We were all called to be self-controlled in all areas of our lives—not just certain ones we deem necessary or comfortable. Self-control is essential for living out a life of faith, as it helps maintain balance and peace when faced with difficult decisions.

Think of those moments when you found yourself losing your temper over trivial matters or engaging in behaviors that are not pleasing to God. If we strive for self-control, these moments will be less frequent, and the decisions we make more holy and righteous.

We are tempted to look at self-control as a way to earn God's love or favor in our lives. But the truth is that God already loves us unconditionally and gives us these gifts out of his immense love for us.

The Bible tells us that self-control is a fruit of the Spirit (Galatians 5:22-23) and that it comes from God. We can ask the Holy Spirit to help increase our own capacity for self-control and to fill our hearts and minds with His wisdom so that we can live out a life of holiness.

Several characters within the pages of the Bible can give us examples of self-control:

Joseph and Daniel – Joseph and Daniel maintained their faith in God even when faced with difficult situations. They chose to focus on the greater good of honoring God through their words and actions rather than pleasing themselves or those around them. Their self-control amid difficult circumstances is an example that we can all strive to follow.

David – David was able to control his emotions and actions during a difficult time of betrayal and loss, even when the people around him were giving in to despair and rage. He chose to remain humble, prayerful, and faithful—despite the pain he felt. His example of self-control is one we can all follow.

Esther – Esther demonstrated tremendous self-control throughout her life by taking bold steps to protect her people and her faith in God. She was able to keep her focus on the greater good of honoring God and serving his people rather than seeking personal gain or comfort from those around her.

Jesus is our most remarkable example of self-control. He continually put the will of God and others before his own, even when it cost him greatly. His example shows us that self-control is not only a way to live out our faith but also a way to be closer to God. He shows us that when we seek to bring glory to God through our actions, our self-control can lead us into a deeper relationship with Him.

What ways can we begin to grow in our capacity for self-control? It begins with knowing God's will for our lives, seeking to align our actions with His, and making it a part of our daily thoughts. We must also turn to Scripture for guidance in understanding how to live out self-control within our own individual contexts.

We can increase our capacity for self-control by:

- Praying regularly that God will help us grow in self-control

- Practicing mindfulness, focusing on the present moment, and being aware of our thoughts, feelings, and actions

- Being intentional about how we use our time and resources

- Becoming more disciplined in areas such as diet, exercise, study, or work

- Seeking out mentors or role models who demonstrate self-control in their own lives

- Making use of accountability partners and prayer partners who will help us stay on track with our goals.

When we begin to foster self-control in our own lives, we can also begin to foster it in the lives of others. We can begin to live as powerful models for others, showing them that with God's help, they, too, can live with self-control. We can use our example to lead and teach others, helping them to increase their own capacity for self-control.

So, how will you see to increase self-control in your own life today? How can you help to share this gift with others so that faith-based diversity, equity, and inclusion are encouraged in the church and our world?

Ask God to give you a greater capacity for self-control and to help you be an example that leads others to Him!

SCRIPTURES TO MEDITATE ON

Philippians 4:13 - "I can do all things through him who strengthens me."

※ ______________________________

※ ______________________________

Proverbs 16:32 - "Better to be slow to anger than a warrior, and one who controls his temper is better than a conqueror."

※ ______________________________

※ ______________________________

Proverbs 25:28 - "A man without self-control is like a city broken into and left without walls."

- ______________________________
- ______________________________

James 1:19 - "Let every person be quick to hear, slow to speak, and slow to anger."

- ______________________________
- ______________________________

5 STATEMENTS TO MEASURE THE FRUIT OF GENTLENESS

- I have a clear understanding of God's will and am able to use it as a guide in my decisions.
- I can recognize when unhealthy emotions are affecting my actions and am able to pause and make wise choices rather than giving in to those feelings.
- I am aware of how my decisions will affect myself and others, and I strive to make choices that honor God.
- I can maintain focus on long-term goals, even when short-term temptations are present.
- I have the ability to be mindful of the present moment, allowing me to respond with wisdom in difficult situations.

REFLECTION QUESTIONS

1. What areas of my life could use more self-control?

❄ _____

❄ _____

2. How can I increase my capacity for self-control in those areas?

❄ _____

❄ _____

3. Is there someone in my life who has demonstrated positive uses of self-control that I could learn from?

❄ _____

❄ _____

4. When faced with difficult situations, how can I respond with self-control rather than relying on my emotions?

❄ _____

❄ _____

How to Increase Self-Control in...

MYSELF

When seeking to grow in our capacity for self-control, it's important to remember that we can only do so with God's help. As we pray and seek wisdom from Scripture, the Holy Spirit will provide us with strength and peace when faced with difficult situations.

For instance, if you find yourself struggling with anger, rather than allowing your emotions to control you, pray for God's help at that moment. Ask Him to fill you with His peace and grace so that you can respond to the situation in a way that honors Him.

As you begin to become more thoughtful of self-control, it's also important to be intentional about how you use your time and resources. Developing habits such as regular prayer, meditation, and scripture reading can help us stay focused on what matters most – living in a way that honors God.

THE CHURCH

As representatives of Christ's church here on earth, it's important to model positive uses of self-control. This means living with wisdom and grace, even in difficult situations. It also means being intentional about our words and actions when interacting with others – especially those from different backgrounds or opinions.

Our example can also be used to teach younger members of the church about the importance of self-control. Through our words and actions, we can provide a tangible example for them to follow, helping them grow in their capacity for this fruit of the spirit. And this can, in turn, help create a church culture where people of all backgrounds and beliefs can worship together in harmony.

The church should be the first place that showcases what godly self-control looks like - not a place of prejudice, discrimination, or anger. Instead, we should be the first to choose love, understanding, and humility.

THE WORLD

Living in a world that is filled with so many distractions can be difficult for us as we strive to live lives of self-control. Yet, there are still ways we can use our own example to lead others toward godly behavior. Here are a few examples:

1. Exercise self-control with your words. Be mindful of the way you talk about those with different opinions, backgrounds, or beliefs.

2. Use your resources wisely, and donate to charitable causes that are making a difference in our world.

3. Refrain from gossiping and instead seek out ways to positively contribute to conversations.

No matter how small our efforts may seem, every step we take towards more godly behavior is a step in the right direction. As we lead by example, let us be mindful that our goal should always be to glorify God and serve others with love and kindness.

As the world sees our example of self-control, may it be a reminder that God's love is the only force powerful enough to change hearts and bring hope to this world. This fruit is powerful, as it can lead to more understanding, acceptance, and grace in our world.

CLOSING PRAYER

Heavenly Father, thank you for the gift of self-control. We ask that you would guide us as we strive to grow in this area so that our lives may be an example of Your love and grace. Help us to use our words, resources, and actions to make a positive difference in the world around us. We pray this in Jesus' Name, Amen.

DEED &
TRUTH CALL TO
ACTION

DEED & TRUTH
CALL TO ACTION

In times of darkness, be the light. (Matthew 5:14-16)

Dear God, in times of darkness, when the world seems bleak and hopeless, help us to remember that we are the light. Help us to shine bright, like a beacon in the night, guiding others to safety and hope. Give us the strength and courage to stand up for what is right, even when it is difficult. Help us to be a source of comfort and support for those struggling and offer a helping hand to those in need. Let our light shine brightly so that others may see Your love and grace through us. In Jesus name, Amen.

In times of disinformation, be the truth. (Col 3:9-10) (3 John 1:4)

Dear Father, in these times of disinformation and confusion, help us seek and speak the truth. May

we be guided by your wisdom and grace and always strive to be honest and transparent in all we do. Grant us the courage to stand up for what is right and to never compromise our values or beliefs in the face of adversity. Let your light shine through us in a world often shrouded in darkness. We pray for the strength and guidance to always be the truth and to use our words and actions to promote justice, love, and understanding. In Jesus name, Amen.

In times of hate, be love. (1 John 4:20)

Heavenly Father, in a world filled with hate, help us to remember the power of love. Guide us to show compassion and kindness to those around us and give us the strength to stand up against injustice and hate. Help us to spread love in our words and actions and never lose hope in the goodness of humanity. We pray for peace and understanding and the courage to be agents of love in a world that desperately needs it. In Jesus name, Amen.

In times of fear, be courageous. (Joshua 1:9)

Dear Lord, as we face moments of fear and uncertainty, give us the courage to stand strong and trust your guidance. Help us to let go of our anxieties and find peace in your loving embrace. Give us the strength to face our challenges with grace and determination and the wisdom to make decisions that reflect your love and goodness. We trust in your protection and guidance and know that with you by our side, we can overcome any obstacle that comes our way. In Jesus name, Amen.

In times of pain, be comfort. (2 Corinthians 1:4)

Great God, as I go through life, I pray that I may be a source of comfort to those in pain. Help me

always be there for them, listen, and offer words of wisdom and support. Grant me the strength to be present for others in their time of need and be a rock they can lean on. Help me to be kind, compassionate, and understanding and to always be willing to lend a helping hand. Help me be a source of hope and comfort for those hurting. I pray that through my actions, I may help to ease their suffering and bring them peace. In Jesus name, Amen.

In times of war, be peace. (Romans 12:18)

Oh Lord, You are the Prince of Peace. We pray for ourselves that we may have the strength to be peacemakers in our own lives and in the world around us. Help us to let go of fear and anger and embrace love and understanding. Grant us the grace to be instruments of your peace and to bring hope and healing to a world in need. We pray to end the violence and suffering that has affected so many. We pray for the safety and well-being of all those affected by war and the courage and strength to face the challenges ahead. In Jesus name, Amen.

In times of chaos, be still. (Psalm 46:10)

Almighty God, in times of chaos and uncertainty, give us the strength and courage to be still. Help us to trust in Your plan and to find peace in Your presence. Remind us that You are in control and that Your love for us is constant and unwavering. We pray that You will give us the courage to be still amidst the storms of life and to trust in You no matter what comes our way. We know that You are with us always and that nothing can separate us from Your love. In Jesus name, Amen.

In times of uncertainty, be unmovable. (1 Corinthians 15:58)

Dear God, thank you for your grace and for being with us always. In times of uncertainty, we ask for your guidance and strength to help us remain unmovable. Give us the confidence and trust in you to navigate through difficult situations and the wisdom to make good decisions. Help us remember that your love and care never waver and that we can always find peace and comfort in your presence. We trust in your goodness and faithfulness and pray that you will continue to bless and guide us in all things. In your precious name, we pray, In Jesus name, Amen.

We can choose to respond to any situation with love and understanding without compromising our faith. Unity and truth are not mutually exclusive. It's time for people on different "sides" of polarizing issues to extend grace to each other for the cause of Christ. Followers of Jesus Christ can no longer be consumed by secular events and processes. We must focus our eyes on eternity.

ADDITIONAL RESOURCES:

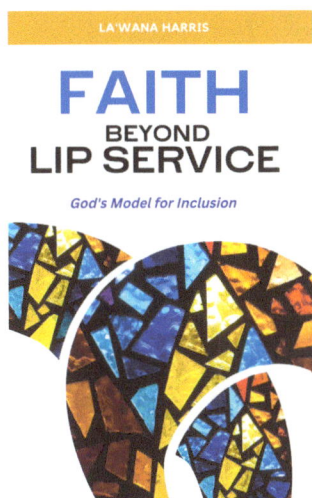

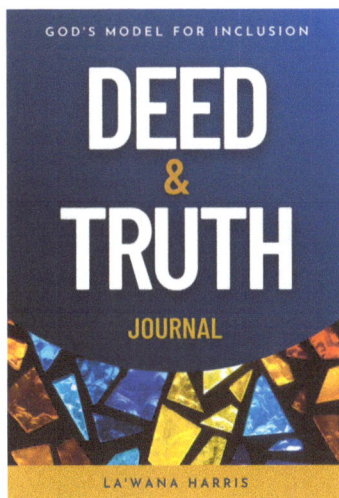

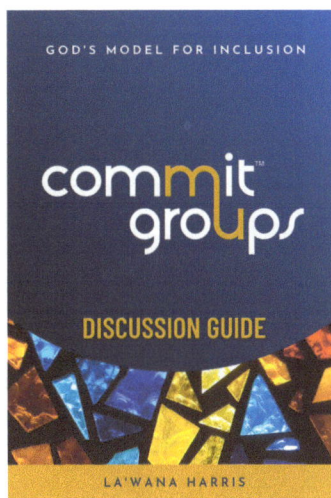

Recommended reading:

Live Dead Journal by Dick Brogden

Operation World: The Definitive Prayer Guide to Every Nation by Jason Mandryk

ABOUT THE AUTHOR:

La'Wana Harris, CDE, ACC, Harris is a Certified Diversity Executive, an ICF Credentialed Coach, and a global leadership development professional who has over 20 years experience in large multinational pharmaceutical companies. Her most recent book, Faith Beyond Lip Service introduces a Christ-centered approach to diversity, equity, and inclusion.

La'Wana is following her calling from God to share practical resources to help bring healing and reconciliation to the body of Christ. She is a Rapid Response Chaplain with the Billy Graham Evangelistic Association, a missionary to Haiti, and has decades of experience in children's ministry and street evangelism.

La'Wana has also demonstrated success in strategizing various academic and corporate functions, including global leadership and organizational development, diversity and inclusion, and people leadership.

She is an adjunct faculty member at the University of Pennsylvania in the Organizational Dynamics program.

La'Wana is also a respected humanitarian and philanthropist. Understanding how important it is for children to read books with characters they can relate to, she created two book series featuring children of color. These books promote cultural diversity and are translated into the native languages of underserved nations. In addition, La'Wana has donated 10,000 books in Haitian Creole to schools and orphanages throughout Haiti in partnership with Grace International. Through her efforts, U.S. sales from these books help support young females entering careers in STEM.

A servant leader, foreign and domestic missionary, and passionate follower of Jesus Christ, La'Wana believes in meeting people where they are to share the gospel with love and compassion.

Printed in the USA
CPSIA information can be obtained
at www.ICGtesting.com
JSHW042004160824
68170JS00003B/5